BLACK&DECKER®

The Complete Guide

Build Your Kids a
Treehouse

Philip Schmidt

**Creative Publishing
international**

CHANHASSEN, MINNESOTA
www.creativepub.com

Creative Publishing international

Copyright © 2007
Creative Publishing international, Inc.
18705 Lake Drive East
Chanhassen, Minnesota 55317
1-800-328-3895
www.creativepub.com
All rights reserved

Printed at R. R. Donnelley

10 9 8 7 6 5 4 3
Library of Congress
Cataloging in Publication on file

President/CEO: Ken Fund

Home Improvement Group
Publisher: Bryan Trandem
Senior Editor: Mark Johanson
Managing Editor: Tracy Stanley

Senior Design Manager: Brad Springer
Design Managers: Jon Simpson, Mary Rohl
Production Artist: Dave Schelitzche

Director of Photography: Tim Himsel
Lead Photographer: Steve Galvin
Photo Coordinators: Julie Caruso, Joanne Wawra
Shop Manager: Randy Austin

Production Managers: Laura Hokkanen, Linda Halls

Author: Philip Schmidt
Project Designer: John Drigot
Page Layout Artist: Kari Johnston
Illustration: Jon Simpson
Photographer: Joel Schnell

THE COMPLETE GUIDE - BUILD YOUR KIDS A TREEHOUSE
Created by: The Editors of Creative Publishing international, Inc., in cooperation with Black & Decker.
Black & Decker® is a trademark of The Black & Decker Corporation and is used under license.

Contents

Build Your Kids a Treehouse

Introduction

Humans are instinctively domestic. From the first months of life we begin building our own special places for play and hiding out. Starting with blankets hung from furniture, you work up to a decorated refrigerator box, then on to outdoor forts made of scrap wood and tarps. Next thing you know, your secret lair for hunkering down is a centrally heated great room with cream carpeting. Comfy, sure, but not the kind of environment that stirs the imagination. And definitely not a treehouse.

A treehouse is the ultimate un-house. For kids, it's a room that never has to be cleaned. A place for muddy shoes and bug jars and a pocketknife stuck into the wall. A house that you can paint whenever and however you want, without gaining approval. For adults, it's a room that never has to be cleaned, a place for muddy shoes and...well, you get the idea. But best of all a treehouse is up in a tree. And that's just cool.

There's a unique feeling you get simply being off the ground supported by a natural structure that grew there. It brings out your animal senses and makes you satisfied just listening to the breezes or studying an insect making its way up the bark. You are lord over all you survey, yet you are welcome to nap at your leisure. Perched and secluded, you are free of terrestrial cares, answering only to the open sky.

Sound good? Then let's get started. This book walks you through the whole process. First you'll select a tree (or trees). Don't worry if your yard isn't blessed with the perfect specimen; there's help for the arboreally challenged. Moving on to the design phase, you'll consider the options—giving the tree a healthy say—then scratch your head and forge your dreams into a workable plan. Then, after a brief safety lesson, you'll harness up, tie off, and start swinging hammers (not saws). Soon your dream house will be under your feet, or above your head, depending on your position.

Don't forget that building a treehouse is a great project for sharing with kids, no matter who plans to use the finished product. Kids are also more likely to enjoy a house if they helped with creating it. In today's hands-off world of outsourcing, it's a great opportunity for them to learn some basic construction skills.

So, what are you waiting for? Get up there!

Special bonus: Six complete treehouse plans.
See page 116.

Portfolio of Treehouses

Just as no two trees are exactly alike, no two treehouses are precisely the same in every detail. In fact, you'll find as much if not more variety among houses in trees as you'll find among the trees themselves. This diversity of design has a lot to do with diversity of builders. Treehouses tend to inspire our innate creativity and grant us license to have fun in a way that terrestrial houses and garages don't. On the following few pages you'll find a stunning portfolio that is a testament to the diversity and creativity that surround the treehouse. From bright and whimsical to subdued and relaxed, you'll find a wealth of themes, motifs, styles and ideas that will inform and inspire you in your treehouse pursuit.

The bigger the tree the more options you'll have for designing and attaching a treehouse. Here, a colorful lookout tower with a ramp and climbing net simply piggybacks onto one side of a mature oak tree.

(Above) Vibrant colors and fun shapes add whimsy and playfulness to this treehouse, which also features a unique limb penetration through a sidewall.

(Left) Treehouses and spaceships often share some design features, contributing to the out-of-this-world appeal of a fort in the trees. Despite appearances, the structure beneath this treehouse is a shed, not an outhouse. (But if it were an outhouse, note that the builder sited it, appropriately, beneath the treehouse, not above it.)

A secret garden in the trees will delight and charm anyone, providing fertile ground for storybook dreams.

(Above) Build your own door to capture precisely the feeling you want your treehouse to put forth. (Besides, a treehouse is no place for fancy manufactured millwork you buy from the design store.)

(Left) Rustic appeal is created by using logs and limbs instead of lumber to build your treehouse. Be aware, though, that some municipalities may not allow this practice.

(Left) A treehouse can become part of a tree. By following the flow of the tree limbs as you design and build, you may find that the tree steers you in intriguing directions.

(Above) Four seasons of fun can be enjoyed in your treehouse, as long as your coats and mittens are up to the task.

(Right) Keeping it simple is a solid approach to treehouse design. A plain treehouse is a blank slate for the imagination.

(Above) Extra support from a set of posts can let you install a relatively large treehouse in a relatively small tree.

(Far left) A pair of trees roughly the same size provide solid support for a treehouse that's nestled between them.

(Left) Common house styles can be adapted to your treehouse design with pleasing effect, as with the chalet-inspired treehouse seen here.

"House" can mean many things in a tree. A roof may be a canopy of branches and a wall could be bright boards and string. Do check with your local building department before following your fancy too far, however. The rope railings seen here would be red-flagged by a lot of inspectors.

(Above) A treehouse is a fortress of fun even with siding from bark slabs and a tar paper roof. In fact, these simple materials have a beauty all their own that many designers find appealing.

(Left) A climbing net and a sturdy platform in a sprawling tree spell big fun for one lucky family.

With a platform in place, a tree structure is ready for use. You may wish to add walls and a roof as you go to spread out the work and allow you to adapt to actual needs and preferences as your kids grow.

A treehouse has an inside, too, and like the exterior it can be as simple or as complex as you choose. The photos on this page depict a treehouse that's definitely on the more finished side, with sleeping bunks, hardwood flooring and even electricity.

(Above) An elevated house in the trees with an independent post support system has the appeal of a tree-built treehouse but without many of the structural limitations.

(Right) What better place for a dreamy deck than outside the front door of your treehouse?

(Right) Shingle styling and a compact Cape Cod design lend the flavor of old Nantucket to this treehouse (even though it happens to be located in Saint Paul, Minnesota).

(Below) An enclosed staircase inside the adjoining fort provides sheltered access to the gangway and the lookout perch.

If all the world's indeed a stage, this tree-based theater/playhouse fits right in (and what a perfect venue for the Neighborhood Kid Players production).

A well-designed, well-built treehouse can completely change your outlook on growing up.

How to Build a Treehouse

Treehouse Basics & Design

The design process for treehouses is often a bit more freewheeling than it may be for terrestrial structures. In fact, the traditional way to design a treehouse (and a technique still used frequently today) is basically to climb up into a tree with boards and fasteners and start to build, making it up as you go along. One of the great attributes of treehouses is that there are very few rules. But the rules that do exist are important ones. And even experienced treehouse builders spend time up-front learning the rules, assessing the needs of the treehouse occupants and performing one of the most critical design tasks: choosing the best tree.

Choosing a Tree

Daydreaming aside, finding your host tree is the first real step in the treehouse process. This is because the tree will have the most say in the final design of the treehouse. More ambitious treehouse plans require healthier trees. In the end, if your host tree isn't up to the task, you'll have to consider a smaller treehouse or figure in some posts for structural support.

Lots of treehouses are hosted by multiple trees. This is usually a good idea from a strength standpoint. However, designing the house can be a lot like working by committee, since trees, like people, tend to act independently when the going gets tough. For most treehouse builders, the selection process isn't a question of which tree to use but rather, "Will old Barkey in our backyard support a treehouse?" For them, the health test is crucial. You don't want to kill your one, beloved tree by burdening it with a temporary structure.

This chapter provides some general tips and rules to help you find a suitable host for your dream house. But before you start, there's this advice (it won't be the last time you hear it): When in doubt, ask an arborist. They're in the phone book, they're not expensive, and they can advise you on everything from tree diagnosis to healthy pruning to long-term maintenance.

Measure the circumference of potential host trees for your treehouse to determine if the tree is big enough for the job. To support a treehouse, a single tree should be at least 5 ft. in circumference.

General Tree Health

A tree doesn't have to be in the absolute prime of its life to be a suitable host, but it must be healthy. Asking a tree how it's been feeling lately probably won't teach you much, so you have to take a holistic approach by piecing together some standard clues. Other factors, such as location, can rule out a candidate more decisively.

Age

Mature trees are best. They're bigger, stronger, and move less in the wind than young ones. They also have more heartwood (the hard, inner core of dead wood). When you drive a lag screw into a tree, it's the heartwood that really offers gripping power.

Roots

For some reason people don't like the sight of exposed roots at the base of a tree. So they cover them with dirt and flower beds. This is like burying someone at the beach and forgetting to stop at their neck. It suffocates the tree roots and can affect the health of the whole tree. If your tree's root flares are buried from re-grading or gardening, take it as a warning sign that there might be problems below.

Another thing to check for is girdling, where newer roots—often from nearby plants—have grown around the tree's primary anchoring roots, cutting off their life supply. Trees next to unpaved driveways or heavily trodden paths may have suffered damage from all the traffic; another warning sign.

To make sure your tree's foundation stays healthy, don't grow grass or add soil over the root flares. Keep shrubs and other competing plants outside of the ground area defined by the reach of the branches. And by all means, keep cars and crowds off the base roots, especially on trees with shallow root systems (see Species Chart, on page 27).

Branches/Limbs at 90° are strongest

Low, stout limbs or relatively bare trunk

Straight trunk

Full, green canopy
Root flares (base roots) with natural exposure and no compaction damage

Trunk, Branches & Leaves (or Needles)

Inspect the largest members of the tree—the trunk and main branches. Look for large holes and hollow spots, rot on the bark or exposed areas, and signs of bug infestation. Check old wounds and damaged areas to see how the tree is healing. Avoid trees with a significant lean, as they are more likely to topple in a storm.

TIP: When you're building the treehouse and drilling holes for anchor screws, pay attention to the wood chips pulled out by the bit: granulated, dusty material indicates rot inside the tree and should be investigated further. Look for clean spirals and tough flakes or chips.

Trees with multiple trunks often are fine for building in; however, the trunk junction is vulnerable to being pulled apart, especially under the added stress of a treehouse. The recommended remedy for this is to bind the tree up above with cables to prevent the trunks from spreading. This is a job for an arborist.

When it comes to branches, look for stout limbs that meet the trunk at a near-perpendicular angle. Typically, the more acute the angle, the weaker the connection, although several suitable tree species naturally have branches set at 45°. Dead branches here and there typically aren't a problem. These can, and should, be cut off before you start building.

Finally, look at the canopy. In spring and summer the leaves should be green and full with no significant bare spots. Needles on evergreen trees should look normal and healthy.

Building in a group of trees is a good way to gain adequate support for a treehouse, but it comes with the added challenge of dealing with multiple forces.

Is It Big Enough?

Well, that depends on how big a house you want. The truth is, in the end, you'll have to be the judge of what your tree can safely support. Here are some general guidelines for assessing tree size, assuming the tree is mature and healthy and the treehouse is a moderately sized (100 sq. ft. or so), one-story affair:

- A single tree that will be the sole support for the house should measure at least five feet in circumference at its base.
- Main supporting limbs (where each limb supports one corner of the house's platform) should be at least 6" in diameter (19" circumference).
- The bigger the tree, the less it will move in the wind, making it a more stable support for a treehouse.
- Different types and shapes of trees have different strength characteristics—a professional's assessment of your tree can help you plan accordingly.

Location

Other important considerations for siting your treehouse are where the tree sits on your property, and what sits around the tree. The wrong location can immediately rule out a tree as a good host.

Let's start with the neighbors. If the tree is too close to your neighbor's property line, thus making your treehouse all too visible, they might complain to the authorities. Soon there's a guy on your doorstep with one of those official-looking metal clipboard boxes full of citation papers and other things you hate to see your name on. Of course, your neighbors might not care what you do, but it's best to talk with them now rather than later. Also, building too close to your property line may involve the authorities simply because you're breaking setback laws of the local zoning code (see page 29).

Trees located on a steep hillside may be too stressed already to handle the added weight and wind resistance of a treehouse. Likewise, trees at water's edge are likely to be unstable and may be fighting a constant battle with erosion.

Treehouses in plain view of roads, paths, or other public byways are begging for trouble because people are fascinated by treehouses. Motorists driving by might be distracted, and kids and teenagers walking by may be tempted to explore (or trash) the house.

Other hazards to look for: nearby power lines or utility poles, roofs or chimneys that come close to the treehouse site, and fences and other potentially dangerous obstacles in the "fall line" underneath the treehouse. Any parent knows how creatively kids court danger. Try not to make it too easy for them.

(Top) Cars, kids, and pets don't always mix well. Avoid trees near roads and busy pathways.

(Above) Trees tend to grow. Take into consideration the proximity of utility lines.

(Right) Trees close to water are vulnerable to erosion and will require constant adult supervision. Consider trees that have a fence between children and water.

Behavior

How your tree acts when the wind blows will become a critical factor in many of your design decisions. That's why, at this selection stage, it's wise to rule out any tree that moves too much. You should never try to weather a storm from inside a treehouse. However, the house itself has no choice but to stay put.

Get to know the tree. If there's a wild branch that likes to swing like a scythe in the wind, you'll have to plan around it, restrain it in a healthy manner, or (if necessary) chop it off. The problem of high winds is only compounded when you build in multiple trees where independent movement of individual trees can exert some nasty opposing forces on your little dream house. Tree movement is a basic reality of treehouse construction, and there are effective methods for dealing with it. The more you know about the tree, the better you can design your house to get along with its host in all conditions.

Treeschool ▸

As a treehouse builder, it's important to understand the inner workings of your benevolent host. This not only builds respect for some of nature's oldest living things, it will also help you decide the best and healthiest ways to build in the tree—where to place screws, support cables, posts, etc. And yes, there may be a quiz.

Tree Anatomy

All eyes to the illustration at right. Now then, a tree trunk and branches have four main layers. The innermost layer is the **heartwood**, made up of dead cells that form a hard, strong core that helps support the tree. Next, the **sapwood** is living fibrous tissue that carries sap (water and nutrients) from the roots to the leaves. Surrounding the sapwood is a thin layer of growing tissue called the **cambium.** It helps develop new wood and the inner bark layer. Finally, the bark is the outer layer of dead cells that protects the inner layers. Underneath the familiar rough layer of bark (called **cork**) is a soft inner bark—the **phloem**—which carries food from the leaves to the rest of the tree.

As you can see, the tree's main food supply channels lie close to the surface. That's why you must minimize any damage to the outer layers. Removing the bark exposes the tree to infection, while cutting into the phloem layer stops the vertical flow of food. One of the worst things you can do to a tree is to cut a ring around the trunk or a branch, or even bind it tightly with rope or cable. This stops all circulation to the rest of the tree.

How a Tree Grows

A tree grows taller through the ends of the trunk and branches. That means that big lower limbs—the kind that are good supports for houses—stay at the same elevation. Trunks and branches also grow in diameter, thanks to the cambium. How much growth depends on the tree, but as a general rule, always leave a 1" to 2" gap around tree parts when encircling them with framing and decking.

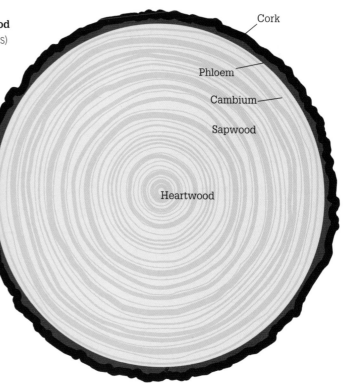

Grooming the Winner

Once you've selected the best candidate it's time to get it prettied up for the big event. A routine pruning is a good idea, but don't start hacking off healthy limbs to make room for a backyard McMansion (see Proper Pruning, below). Get rid of dead branches in the tree and clear the ground underneath. If you'd like a soft ground cover beneath (a recommended kid-safety measure), cover the area with several inches of wood chips, preferably from the same species of tree. Don't cover the area with soil.

Later, when you have a better idea of the size of your treehouse, make sure the structure won't be blocking the roots' source of rainwater. If it will, find out how much and how often you'll need to water the tree to compensate.

PROPER PRUNING ▸

The best tool for pruning is a telephone. Use it to call an arborist and have them assess the tree and make the appropriate cuts. If you do decide to go it alone, be careful, and follow these basic rules:

1. Never cut away more than 1/3 of the tree's branches.
2. Start with a shallow undercut several inches away from the branch bark collar—the bulge where the branch meets the trunk. The undercut ensures the bark doesn't peel off as the branch drops.
3. Complete the cut from the top to remove the bulk of the branch.
4. Make a final cut flush with the outside of the branch bark collar. Do not cut into the collar.
5. Leave the wound to heal itself. Don't paint it or add any kind of sealant or preservative.

Start by undercutting from beneath the limb with your bow saw or chain saw.

Finish the cut from above—this keeps the bark from tearing when the limb breaks loose.

Trim the stub from the limb so it's flush with the branch collar.

Choosing a Tree Species

GOOD TREES
DECIDUOUS (BROADLEAF) TREES

Characteristics	Native Area	Average Height
Oak		
Strong, durable, low branches	**White Oak:** California	50-90 ft.
	Live Oak: Gulf coastal & Atlantic plains; central Texas	40-50 ft.
	Northern Red: eastern US and north into Canada	60-80 ft.
Maple		
Sugar Maple is preferred over Red, but both are good hosts	**Sugar Maple:** northeastern US, north into Canada	60-80 ft.
	Red Maple: eastern half of US, north into Canada	50-70 ft.
Beech		
Smooth bark, horizontal branches	Eastern US; southeastern Canada	60-80 ft.
Apple		
Low, stout branches	Most of US; southern Canada	20-30 ft.
Ash		
Strong, straight trunk; should be carefully checked for disease	Eastern half of US; southeastern Canada	60-80 ft.

EVERGREEN (NEEDLELEAF) TREES

Characteristics	Native Area	Average Height
Douglas Fir		
Long-living; large, mature trunks have few low branches	Pacific coast; US and Canadian Rocky Mountains	180-250 ft.
Pine		
Fast-growing; branches often numerous but small and flexible	**Ponderosa Pine:** western half of US; British Columbia	100-180 ft.
	Eastern White Pine: northeastern, Great Lakes, and Appalachian regions of US	75-100 ft.
	Sugar Pine: California, Oregon, western Nevada	175-200 ft.
Spruce		
Can be prone to infestation; shallow roots	**Black Spruce:** Alaska; Canada; northeastern US	30-40 ft.
	Engelmann Spruce: Pacific Northwest; Rocky Mountain states	100-120 ft.
Hemlock		
Immature trees may have little trunk exposure	Great Lakes and Appalachian regions of US; southeastern Canada	60-75 ft.

NOT-SO-GOOD TREES

	Drawbacks
Cottonwood	Soft, spongy wood
Birch	Short lifespan, weak branches
Poplar & Aspen	Shallow roots, short lifespan
Black Walnut	Branches are brittle and break easily

Some of the elements that may be regulated by your local building code and zoning laws include: Size restriction—square footage of floor plan • Height restriction—from ground to top of treehouse • Railing height and baluster spacing • Setback—how closely you can build to your property line

Planning & Design

If you built a treehouse as a kid you probably didn't spend a lot of time planning it beforehand. You had plenty of ideas and knew what you wanted—a trap door, a lookout post, a tire swing, and maybe a parachuting platform or helicopter pad—you just weren't exactly sure how everything would come together. In the end, you decided to figure it out along the way and got started.

Of course, some people might use the same approach today (good luck on the helicopter pad), but be advised that a little planning up front could save your project from disaster. Remember the guy with the metal clipboard from the city office? You don't want him showing up with a demolition order just as you're nailing up the last piece of trim.

This chapter will get you thinking about general design features, such as the size and style of the treehouse, where it will sit in the tree, and how you'll get from the ground to the front door—if you want a front door. In this section we cover the all-important construction details, like anchoring to the tree and building the platform, walls, and roof. Inevitably there's plenty of give-and-take between design dreams and structural necessity. But that's what makes treehouse building such a fun and satisfying challenge.

NOTE: Before refining your treehouse plans, see Treehouse Safety (page 50) for important safety-related design considerations.

Building Codes & Zoning Laws

It's time to pinch your nose and swallow the medicine. The sooner you get it over with, the sooner you can go out and play. By checking into the building and zoning rules for your area you can avoid the mistake of spending time on elaborate plans only to run into a brick wall of bureaucracy.

When it comes to building codes and treehouses, the official word is that there is no official word. Many municipalities—the governing powers over building and zoning laws—consider treehouses to be "temporary" structures when they fit within certain size limits, typically about 100-120 square ft. and not more than 10-12 ft. tall. If you have concerns about the restrictiveness of the local laws, keeping your treehouse within their size limits for temporary structures is a good precaution to take.

It's often likely that city officials consider treehouses too minor to be concerned with them. On top of that, building codes for earth-bound buildings are based on measurable, predictable factors that engineers use to calculate things like strength requirements. Drafting a set of standards for structures built on living, moving, and infinitely variable foundations (trees) quickly becomes a cat-herding exercise for engineers. Thus, few codes exist that set construction standards for treehouses. This means more responsibility is placed on the builder.

When it comes to zoning laws, the city planning office is concerned less with a treehouse's construction and more with its impact on your property. They may state that you can't build anything within 3 ft. or more of your property line (called setback restriction) or that you can't build a treehouse in your front yard (the Joneses might not be the treehouse type).

The bottom line is this: Your local planning office might require you to get a building permit and pass inspections for your treehouse, or they might not care what you do, provided you keep the building within specific parameters. It's up to you to learn the rules.

Although city laws are all over the place regarding treehouses, here are a few tips that might help you avoid trouble with your treehouse:

• Talk with your neighbors about your treehouse plans. A show of respect and diplomacy on your part is likely to prevent them from filing a complaint with the authorities. It also smooths the way for later when you have to borrow tools for the project.

• Be careful where you place windows (and decks) in your treehouse. Your neighbors might be a touch uncomfortable if you suddenly have a commanding view of their hot tub or a straight shot into their second-story windows.

• Electricity and, especially, plumbing services running to a treehouse tell the authorities that you plan to live there, thus your house crosses a big line from "temporary structure" to "residence" or "dwelling" and becomes subject to all the requirements of the standard building code.

• Don't build in a front-yard tree or any place that's easily viewed from a public road. The point is not to hide from the authorities, it's that conspicuous treehouses attract too much attention for the city's comfort, and the house might annoy your neighbors.

• In addition to keeping the size of your house in check, pay attention to any height restriction for backyard structures. Treehouses can easily exceed these, for obvious reasons, but nevertheless may be held to the same height limits as sheds, garages, etcetera.

• Even if the local building laws don't cover treehouses, you can look to the regular building code for guidance. It outlines construction standards for things like railings, floor joist spans, and accommodations for local weather and geologic (earthquake) conditions. With appropriate adaptations for the treehouse environment, many of the standards established for ground-houses will work for your perched palace.

If you're building a treehouse for kids to use or share with the adults, include them in the design process. Many a parent has gone to great lengths to surprise kids with a fancy treehouse that ultimately doesn't get used. It's like gifting a young child with an exquisite toy only to find that their favorite part is the ribbon on the box.

Not only will kids get more pleasure from a house they help to create, but by finding practical solutions to bring their creative ideas to life, they also will learn the essence of architecture. Who knows, you might have another Frank Lloyd Wright on your hands, or better yet for treehouses, another Christopher Wren.

Encourage creativity by soliciting ideas from all of your family members and try to work the ideas into the final plan.

Elements of a Treehouse

Treehouses can range in style from miniature versions of traditional houses to funky masterpieces of original inspiration. Of course, your ideal treehouse might be nothing more than a lofty hammock slung above a pine deck. Personal taste is what it's all about. Here are some design options to get you thinking.

Walls

Walls define the look and shape of a house and do more than any other element to create the feel of the interior space. A treehouse can have solid walls for privacy and a greater sense of enclosure, or it can open up to the elements and let the tree define its boundaries. If you'd like both options, consider an awning-style wall with a hinged top section that flips open.

Enclosed walls, either full height or stub walls like these, block or partially block views into the neighbors' yard and create a secret room for kids.

Open walls admit breezes and allow unobstructed views, plus they're easier and cheaper to build than enclosed walls. If you choose not to build walls, build safety railings instead.

Flip-up wall panels let you open up a section of the roof for airflow when you don't need to batten down for shelter.

Round or curved walls blend naturally with the shape of a tree.

Roofs

Treehouse roofs can take on almost any shape and often exhibit a combination of styles. Incorporating branches and trunks into the roof design makes for interesting, organic forms. A common approach to designing a roof is to start with a traditional style then improvise as needed to fit your house. Or, you might decide to skip the roof altogether, preferring the shelter of the tree's canopy rather than boards and shingles.

Shed roofs have an easy-to-build, flat shape, making them a good choice for all types of treehouses.

Gable roofs are considered the most classic roof style, with angled wall sections at either end.

A removable roof made from canvas or a plastic tarp may be all you need to shelter a tree fort or sun deck.

Hip roofs are sloped on all sides and are more difficult to frame than sheds and gables.

A conical roof is an impressive way to top a rounded wall. They're built with closely spaced rafters fanning out from the roof peak.

Windows & Doors

The best doors and windows to use on treehouses are either found or homemade. It's fun to design a wall or entryway around salvaged materials—maybe a reclaimed ship's porthole window or a creaky, old cellar door. You could use new, factory-made units, but their large size and polished appearance don't fit most treehouses. Kids especially love playful designs, such as Dutch doors, with swinging top and bottom halves, or little peek-a-boo openings through which they can demand, "Who goes there?!"

Architectural salvage shops are full of interesting finds for windows and doors.

Simple homemade windows are easy to make with plastic glazing and scrap lumber.

Dutch doors offer a fun change of pace that kids (and adults) find charming.

A solid door with a padlock may be a good idea, if not necessary, for securing a remote treehouse.

Access Options

Perhaps the best thing about a treehouse is all the cool stuff that you can't have in a real house, like trap doors and cargo nets and fireman's poles. And who needs a front door when you can exit SWAT-style down a climbing rope? Okay, not everyone is the right age for the Ninja lifestyle. A sturdy ladder or even a staircase are also perfectly respectable modes for accessing a treehouse. But just to be safe you might want to include a secret escape hatch and zip line... in case of an alien air assault.

(Above) Ladders provide safe and easy access while maintaining a sense of remoteness.

(Right) Stairs are a good, practical option for multi-use and multi-user treehouses.

Decks

One of the most popular treehouse designs includes a house covering about ½ to ⅔ of its supporting platform, leaving the rest open for a small deck or sitting porch. This is a nice way to provide both open and enclosed spaces for your lofty getaway. A small deck in front makes a good, safe landing for a staircase or access ladder, while a large deck can be the perfect spot for having a drink with friends at sunset.

With the platform in place, it's easy to make room for a tree deck.

Centering a small house on a platform makes an instant wraparound deck.

Stairs or a ladder require a top landing; adding a foot or two of space to the landing lets it double as a sitting area.

Design Considerations

Ask any treehouse nut about design and you're bound to be advised to let the tree lead the way. This means respecting the tree's natural strengths and weaknesses and not over-stressing it with an unsuitable or excessive house design. It also speaks to aesthetics. Much of a treehouse's appeal comes from its host, and the best house designs complement the tree's character or make use of special natural features. Designing within the branches, as it were, is also good treehouse philosophy and makes the planning and construction—not to mention the enjoyment—of your house as fun as it should be.

So, now that you've picked a tree and had a talk with the folks at the local planning office, it's time to give your house some shape, in your mind at least. As you mull over the height, size, and features of your new home, don't be afraid to make sketches of your ideas—despite what we've all been told, doodling during work is actually a good thing. This will also help with the final step of the design process—making scaled drawings.

It doesn't take much elevation for kids to get that lofty feeling in their own treehouse.

Platform Height

The first big decision to make is how high to set the treehouse. If it will be used by kids, keep the platform no more than 6 to 8 ft. above the ground. Any higher is dangerous, and kids will have just as much fun at 6 ft. as they would at 12 or 20 ft. If your treehouse is designed mostly for adults, you can go higher, but before deciding ask yourself:

- Will you need easy access? If you're using the house as an office or studio, consider the difficulty of hauling up supplies (and lunch).
- Is construction feasible? Building a treehouse is generally the most potentially hazardous aspect of treehouse life. Also, construction could be slowed considerably by a very high platform.
- Will neighborhood kids be able to climb up into the house? If so, you could be courting trouble with a lofty placement.

Regardless of where you build, you must make sure the treehouse placement is good for the tree. Arborists recommend building below the tree's center of gravity. This is something you'll just have to get a feel for, based on the tree's size and behavior. One general guideline is to build in the lowest 1/3 of the tree's overall height. If you're lucky, your host tree will make it easy for you and have a perfect open cradle of stout limbs at just the right height. Alas, it's usually not that obvious.

Another consideration is pruning the tree to make room for your house. While thoughtful, therapeutic pruning is good, and recommended by tree experts, removing large, healthy limbs to pave the way for easy construction is really straying from the point of building in a tree. If an obstructing limb becomes a deal-breaker for your house plans, consult an arborist to make sure that removing it won't harm the tree.

Finally, give yourself a good, old fashioned visual reference: Climb up in the tree (or onto a ladder) and stand at the proposed platform height. Check out the view and the headroom. Picture yourself lounging like there's no tomorrow. Happy? Good. Now you can decide how to get from the ground to your finished house.

Access

To help determine the means of access, look again to the users of the treehouse. Older, that is mature, people probably would prefer stairs or a comfortable ladder, while kids usually want a more challenging or fun route (just say no to mini-tramps and pole vaulting, however). Do you want a ladder or stairs that are easy to reach from your regular house? Or out of view from the house?

Make sure your planned means of access is viable for the chosen platform height. One mode of access to rule out: steps or rungs individually fastened along the tree trunk. Even when built properly—with threaded screws, not nails—these are fraught with safety problems and require an unnecessary amount of hardware placed into the tree.

Sun & Seasons

As with a regular house, sunlight and weather are important design considerations. Perhaps you've dreamed of waking up with the summer sunrise or climbing into your perch to catch the sunset after a long day at the office. Position your house carefully to make the most of your favorite outdoor hours. For kids, some full shade is a must to avoid prolonged sun exposure.

With deciduous trees, the changing seasons come with a potential shocker. When fall hits and your host tree is suddenly a bare skeleton, your treehouse might stick out like an embarrassing tattoo. Just something to keep in mind if you're building when the tree's canopy is full.

Don't plan on using the familiar nailed-on steps for access. They can easily give way to the side or pull completely out of the tree while you're climbing.

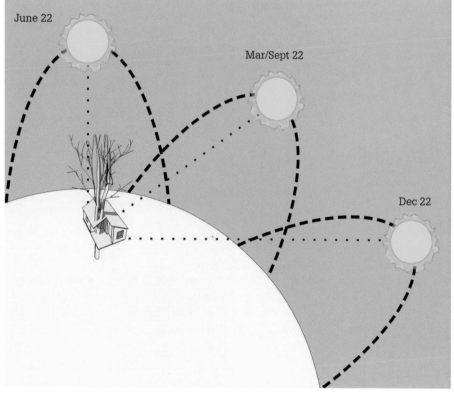

The sun moves from its high point in summer to its low point in winter. Shadows change accordingly. Try and keep the sun in mind as you plan.

Size, Shape & Proportions

Think small. Or at least start by thinking small. Here's why: Weight is an important factor for any treehouse. The larger the house, the greater the weight burden on the tree. A big house will also catch more wind, stressing the branches more than they're used to and generally making it harder for the tree to stay upright. It's not unheard of to have a disproportionately large treehouse create such a windsail that the entire tree blows over. If you feel the need to go big, find a big tree or build in a group of very stable trees.

In treehouses, wall heights don't need to be the standard 8 feet that they are in regular houses. For adults, 6½ feet is a better place to start. This makes the house cozier and more nest-like. The necessary headroom for a kids' treehouse depends on their ages and how long they're likely to use the house. Generally, 6 feet of headroom should give them plenty of room to grow.

To determine how much floor (platform) space you need, try this: Clear out a corner of a room where two walls meet at a right angle, then grab two tape measures. Pull out the tapes and lock them in place at any desired dimensions—for example, set both at 6 ft. for a 36 sq. ft. floor, or set one at 8 ft. and one at 10 ft. for an 80 sq. ft. floor.

Lay the tapes on the floor so they meet at a right angle, representing the two imagined walls of your area. Step inside the area to get a feel for its size. Bring in some chairs and other furniture you might want in the treehouse to see how everything fits. Don't forget to factor in the tree, especially if you're building your platform around the trunk.

Not that your treehouse has to be square. In fact, this is a rare opportunity to build out of square. Why not a triangle or rhombus or something more amoeba-like? There are no points off for ignoring traditional design principles, like symmetry. You already have a house that follows the rules. When it comes to treehouses, quirks and funny angles add character and make it more personal.

Two walls and two tape measures make it easy to visualize how much floor space you'll need.

Sturdy posts make strong treehouse supports, but are recommended only for treehouses with very little potential movement.

Using Posts

Treehouse snobs may balk at the use of support posts, but this is nothing to be ashamed of. Posts offer an effective way to compensate for trees that can't solely support a treehouse or for cases where a design calls for more trees than you have. Posts can also serve to shore up support beams with long spans between trees.

Keep in mind that using posts places limits on the house design. Namely, the house must be close to the ground. This is because the post will be cemented in the ground and essentially immovable, while the tree remains free to sway with the wind. In mature trees, movement typically is minimal in the lowest 10-12% of the tree's total height. Therefore, if you use posts as main support members, and the tree is 60 ft. tall, for example, keep the platform within 6 to 7 ft. of the ground.

Stay Flexible

As a final design tip, keep an open mind to changes. You might find yourself installing the walls when you discover that a window that was supposed to overlook the garden actually gives you a better view of the alley. Or, you might be surprised by the shadows within the canopy and decide to add an opening to bring in more sunlight. Building a treehouse is an organic process. Be ready to adapt.

A floor plan showing the completed platform helps you divide up the floor space and allocate room for decks, landings, and other open areas.

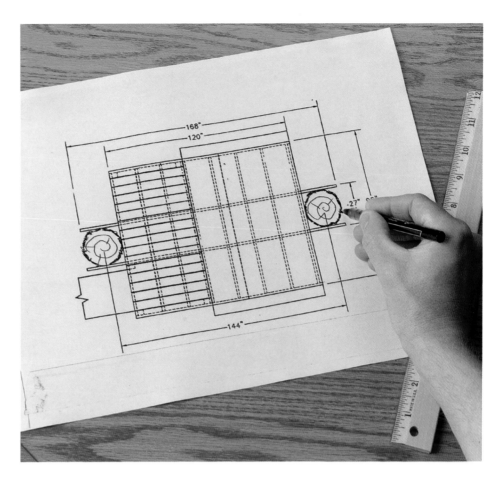

A plan view of the platform framing gives you a birds-eye perspective of the host trees and main treehouse support members.

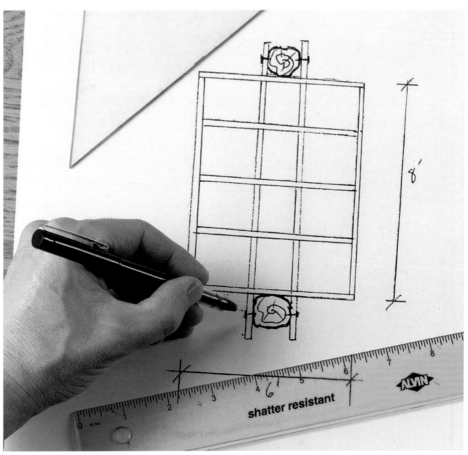

Drawing Plans

Spending a little time testing your ideas on paper almost always pays off when it comes time to build a treehouse. It's a lot easier to make changes to a few pencil lines than a lumber frame screwed to a tree 10 ft. in the air.

Start by taking some measurements of the building site. That is, the host trees. Measure the trunks, main branches, and relative positions of distinguishing marks and features. With those measurements and a little freehand sketching of the tree, you'll be able to make reasonably accurate scale drawings of the tree and treehouse from various perspectives.

Draw the platform first. Getting the platform right is the most challenging part of building a treehouse and usually requires some trial-and-error at the drawing board. If you don't want to make a complete set of plans, at least draw up the platform to test your ideas before you start building.

To experiment with ideas for the walls and roof, take a digital photo of the tree. Print it out at full-page size, then use your measurements of distinguishing features to get a sense of the photo's scale. Lay tracing paper over the photo to sketch your ideas. Take additional photos at different angles to the tree to create the various elevation drawings.

Elevation drawings show the house from various angles. These are helpful for judging proportions and planning for intervening branches, etc. Sketching over digital photo printouts gives you an accurate picture of how the finished project will look in the tree.

Lumber for treehouses must be suitable for outdoor exposure. This includes cedar, redwood, pressure-treated pine, and exterior-grade or marine plywood (not shown).

Lumber & Hardware

The classic kid-built treehouse is made with scrap wood, often "found" at a neighborhood construction site, and rusty nails fished out of a coffee can. Add some tar paper and carpet remnants, and you have yourself an awesome hideaway. It's still a great way to build a treehouse. But if that's what you had in mind, you probably wouldn't be reading this book (you'd be using it as a roof shingle). So what materials should you use on your next treehouse? The short answer is: everything rot-resistant and corrosion-resistant.

For lumber, the most commonly available types of rot-resistant wood are redwood, cedar, and pressure-treated pine (sometimes fir or other species). All of these can withstand years of weather without rotting. Even if your treehouse is kept dry with a sealed roof, it's a good idea to use one of these outdoor wood types on the interior parts as well, because you're bound to get some moisture inside.

When it comes to structural elements, make sure your lumber is strong enough. For example, cedar 2× lumber, if you can find it, isn't as strong as the Southern pine, fir, or larch typically specified in span tables. Redwood heartwood is stronger than redwood softwood but also more expensive. Plywood is another common material in treehouses—always use exterior-grade or marine plywood.

A note about pressure-treated lumber: By law, all lumber now sold for residential use may not be treated with chemicals containing arsenic, previously a common ingredient in many treatment solutions. However, it does contain preservatives that allow a standard piece of wood to stay rot-free for up to 30 years. Something to consider when choosing lumber for high-contact areas like benches, tables, and handrails.

For hardware, a good standard is hot-dipped or drop-forged galvanized steel—available in many types of bolts, screws, and connectors. Aluminum roofing nails are also acceptable. Stainless steel is the best and strongest rust-proof material but comes in a somewhat limited variety of hardware and costs a lot more than galvanized steel.

For any structural connections to the tree, use screws and bolts instead of nails. Bolts should be at least ½" in diameter and always galvanized for corrosion protection (or made of rust-proof material). Nails simply can't be trusted in trees. There's too much movement, and the live wood doesn't hold nails as consistently or predictably as dry lumber does. Galvanized nails are fine for framing connections and general construction of the house parts, although in many cases you might prefer to use deck screws or galvanized wood screws. With the smaller 2 × 2 and 2 × 3 framing used in treehouses, assembly is easier with screws.

Specialty connections and anchoring systems might call for Extra High Strength cable and high-tensile galvanized chain. Another hardware option available through a specialty supplier is the GL treehouse anchor, which screws into the tree's trunk to serve as a heavy-duty limb for supporting platforms (see page 62).

Reclaimed Lumber & Materials

Building a treehouse offers a great opportunity to scrounge around recycled lumber yards and architectural salvage shops for materials like weathered, old timbers and one-of-a-kind fixtures. On top of being a fun scavenger hunt, this is also the best way to "build green." One note of caution, however: Inspect old lumber carefully before using it for structural members. Significant cracks, excessive knots, and evidence of rot are common indications that the wood might not be reliable or strong enough for its intended use.

Commonly Used Hardware for Treehouses

Lag screws

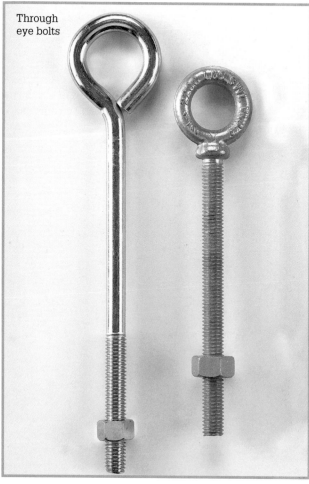

Through eye bolts

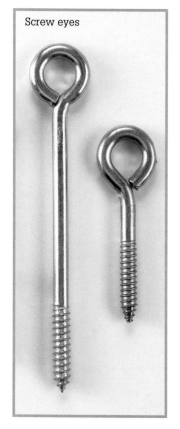

Screw eyes

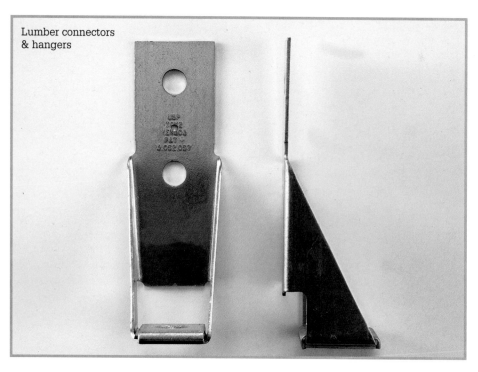

Lumber connectors & hangers

Commonly Used Hardware for Treehouses

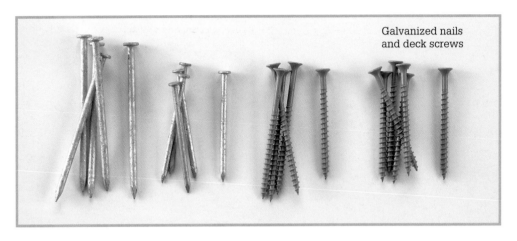

Galvanized nails and deck screws

Galvanized washers

Galvanized high-tensile chain (¾" link)

Pulley

Cable clamps and connectors

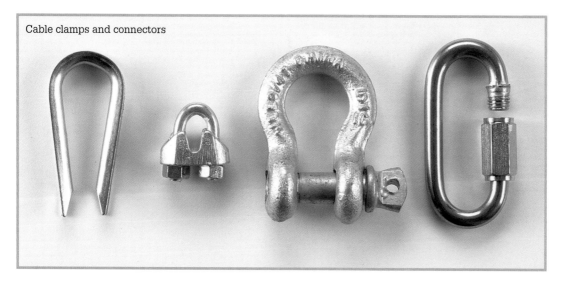

Drill bit

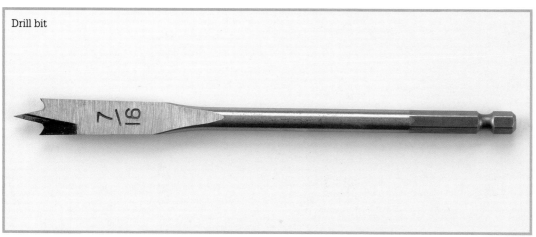

EHS galvanized steel cable

With treehouses, safety is equally important after you're done as when you're doing the building.

Treehouse Safety

The fact is, a house up in a tree comes with some risks. But so does an elevated deck off of your kitchen or a jungle gym in your backyard. What makes you comfortable using these things on a daily basis is your belief that they were designed thoughtfully to prevent common hazards, as well as your own regular maintenance of the structures to ensure their safety. The same applies to treehouses, although treehouses present an additional safety consideration—building off the ground.

Therefore, treehouse safety can be divided into two categories: safe design and safe working conditions. Both are equally important and perfectly manageable, and both should be followed regardless of who uses the house. A kids' treehouse naturally involves more safety concerns than one used exclusively by adults. However, keep in mind that you never know when children might visit, and it's too late once they're up there. It's like bringing a two-year-old into a non-babyproofed home. The adults are suddenly scrambling madly as they discover all the things that are perfectly safe for them but potentially deadly for a toddler.

Safe Treehouse Design

The primary safeguard on any treehouse is the supporting platform. It alone keeps the house and its occupants aloft. Even if every other element is designed to the highest standards, a treehouse is completely unsafe if the platform isn't sound. A later chapter covers platform construction in detail, so for now, just two quick reminders:

1. Keep platforms for kids' treehouses at 8 ft. above the ground or lower.
2. Inspect the platform support members and tree connections regularly to make sure everything's in good shape.

With a strong, stable platform in place, you can turn your attention to the other elements of safety in design.

Everything's riding on the treehouse platform. Be sure to keep it in good condition.

Sound, code-compliant railings are a critical safety feature for treehouse users of all ages.

Railings

Every part of a treehouse platform that isn't bound by walls must have a sturdy railing. Building codes around the country tend to agree on railing specifications, and these are the best rules to follow for treehouses, too.

In general, railings must be at least 36" tall, with vertical balusters no more than 4" apart. A railing should be strong enough to withstand several adults leaning against it at once, as well as roughhousing kids. On treehouses for small children, use only standard 2 × 2 lumber or other rigid vertical balusters, not rope or cable balusters. For kids of all ages, don't use horizontal balusters. These work well for cattle fencing, but kids are too tempted to climb them. See page 93 for more railing specifications and instructions on building railings.

Access Landings

Each type of access to a treehouse—ladder, rope, stairs, etc.—has its own design standards for safety, but all must have a landing point at which to arrive or depart from, the house. In many cases, the landing necessitates a gap in a railing or other opening and thus a potential fall hazard. Keep this in mind when planning access to your treehouse, and consider these recommendations:

- Include a safety rail across openings in railings (this is a must, not an option).
- Leave plenty of room around access openings, enough for anyone to safely climb onto the treehouse platform and stand up without backing up.
- Consider non-slip decking on landings to prevent falls if the surface gets wet.
- Add handles at the sides of access openings and anywhere else to facilitate climbing up and down; handholds cut into the treehouse floor work well, too.
- Install a safety gate to bar young children from areas where there are access openings.

Windows & Doors

The obvious safety hazard for windows and doors is glass. So the rule is: Don't use it, especially in kids' treehouses. Standard glass is too easily broken during play or by swaying branches or rocks thrown by taunted older brothers. Instead, use strong plastic sheeting. The strongest stuff is ¼"-thick polycarbonate glazing. It's rated for outdoor public buildings, like kiosks and bus stops, so it can easily survive the abuse from your own little vandals. Plastic does get scratched and some becomes cloudy over time, but it's easily replaceable and is better than a trip to the emergency room.

Even more important than the glazing is the placement of doors and windows. All doors and operable windows must open over a deck, not a drop to the ground. If a door is close to an access point, make sure there's ample floor space between the door and any opening in a railing, for example.

Ground Below the Tree

Since occasional short falls are likely to occur when kids are climbing around trees, it's a good idea to fill the area beneath your treehouse with a soft ground cover. The best material for the health of the tree is wood chips. A 6"-thick bed of wood chips effectively cushions a fall from 7 feet, according to the National Resource Center for Health and Safety in Child Care. Also, keep the general area beneath the house free of rocks, branches, and anything else one would prefer not to land on.

A sturdy handle is a welcome sight to tired climbers. Make sure all handles and mounting hardware are galvanized or otherwise corrosion-protected.

A soft bed of loose ground cover is recommended under any kids' treehouse or areas where kids will be climbing.

TREEFORT KNOX ▸

Locking up may seem unnecessary for most backyard hideaways, but for some treehouses it's a sensible precaution. For example, treehouses located out of your daily view, especially those near a public road, can attract a lot of negative attention, like vandalism. More important, kids just can't resist getting into stuff, and you don't want to face a lawsuit because you made it easy for them to waltz into your house and get hurt. Of course, you had nothing to do with it. But try telling that to a plaintiff lawyer.

These are just suggestions, not legal advice:

- Install a strong door with a padlock (¾" plywood backed by a lumber frame is a good choice; it may be ugly, but it's strong).
- Post signage stating "No Trespassing," "Private Property," "Danger," or similar warnings.
- Install window shutters that lock on the inside or can be padlocked from the outside.
- Use plastic instead of glass in windows (the polycarbonate glazing mentioned on page 53 won't be broken with rocks).
- Use a retractable or removable ladder as the only means of access, and take it away when you leave the treehouse.

Construction Details

One of the first rules of building children's play structures is to countersink all exposed hardware. For good reason. If you fall and slide along a post, you might get a scrape and some splinters, but you're much better off than if your kneecap hits a protruding bolt on the way down. Follow the countersink rule for all kids' treehouses.

Speaking of splinters, take the time to sand rough edges as you build your house. Your kids and guests will be glad you did. Also keep an eye out for sharp points, protruding nails, and any rusty metal.

Maintenance

Treehouses fight a constant battle with gravity. This, combined with outdoor exposure and the threat of rust and rot make regular inspections of the house a critical safety precaution. Inspect your treehouse several times throughout the year for signs of rot or damage to structural members and all supporting hardware. Also check everything after big storms and high winds, as excessive tree movement can easily cause damage to wood structures or break anchors without you knowing it. Test safety railings, handholds, and access equipment more frequently.

Inspect the tree around connecting points for stress fractures and damage to the bark. Weighted members and tensioned cables and ropes rubbing against the bark can be deadly for a tree if it cuts into the layers just below the bark. Check openings where the trunk and branches pass through the treehouse, and expand them as needed to avoid strangling the tree. Finally, remove dead or damaged branches that could fall on the house.

Neglected support beams and connections are the most common causes of treehouse disasters. Check these parts often for rot, corrosion, and damage.

Working Safely

Off-the-ground work has its own long list of safety guidelines on top of the regular set of basic construction safety rules. Since you can learn about general tool and job site safety anywhere (please do so), the focus here is on matters specific to treehouse building and related gravity-defying feats. But here are some good points to keep in mind.

Working outdoors presents challenges not faced in the interior, such as dealing with the weather, working at heights, and staying clear of power lines. By taking a few common-sense safety precautions, you can perform exterior work safely.

Dress appropriately for the job and weather. Avoid working in extreme temperatures, hot or cold, and never work outdoors during a storm or high winds.

Work with a helper whenever possible—especially when working at heights. If you must work alone, tell a family member or friend so the person can check in with you periodically. If you own a portable phone, keep it with you at all times.

Don't use tools or work at heights after consuming alcohol. If you're taking medicine, read the label and follow the recommendations regarding the use of tools and equipment.

When using ladders, extend the top of the ladder three feet above the roof edge for greater stability. Climb on and off the ladder at a point as close to the ground as possible. Use caution and keep your center of gravity low when moving from a ladder onto a roof. Keep your hips between the side rails when reaching over the side of a ladder, and be careful not to extend yourself too far or it could throw off your balance. Move the ladder as often as necessary to avoid over-reaching. Finally, don't exceed the work-load rating for your ladder. Read and follow the load limits and safety instructions listed on the label.

Hardhat Area (Heads Up!)

The general area underneath the tree should be off limits to anyone not actively working on the project at hand. Someone walking idly underneath to check things out might not be engaged enough to react if something falls. Hard hats are a good idea for anyone working on the project and for kids anywhere close to the job site.

To keep an extension cord from dropping—and sometimes taking your tool with it—wrap the cord around a branch to carry the bulk of the weight. Also, wear a tool belt to keep tools and fasteners within reach while keeping your hands free to grab lumber, etcetera.

During construction, ladder management is an exceptionally important aspect of jobsite safety. Since trees generally do not afford flat, smooth areas for the ladder rungs to rest, adding padded tips will help stabilize the ladder. And remember: a fall of just a couple of feet from a ladder can cause a fractured elbow or worse.

Pulley Systems

A pulley is one of the fun features found on a lot of treehouses. They're great for delivering baskets full of food and supplies. During the build, a simple pulley set up with a bucket or crate is handy for hauling up tools and hardware.

Here's an easy way to set up a simple, lightweight pulley:

1. Using a strong, nylon or manila rope (don't use polypropylene, which doesn't stand up under sun exposure), tie one end to a small sandbag and throw it over a strong branch.

2. Tie a corrosion-resistant pulley near the end of the rope, then tie a loop closer to the end, using bowline knots for both.

3. Feed a second rope through the pulley and temporarily secure both ends so the rope won't slip through the pulley.

4. Thread the first rope through the loop made in step 2, then haul the pulley up snug to the branch. Tie off the end you're holding to secure the pulley to the branch.

For heavy-duty lifting, use a block and tackle (see next page),which is a pulley system that has one rope strung through two sets of pulleys (blocks). The magic of multiple-pulley systems is that the lifting power is increased by 1× for each pulley. For example, a block and tackle with 6 pulleys gives you 6 pounds of lifting force for each pound of force you put onto the pulling rope. If you weigh 150 pounds and hang on the pulling end, you could raise a nearly 900 lb. load without moving a muscle. The drawback is that you have to pull the rope 6x farther than if you were using a single pulley. For a high treehouse, you'll need a lot of rope.

When hauling up loads with a block and tackle, try to have a second person on the ground to man a control line tied to the load. This helps stabilize the load and steer it through branches and other obstacles. Additional control like this makes it safer for those up in the tree.

The bowline is one of the most reliable knots, forming a strong loop that won't slip.

One rope raises and affixes the pulley to the tree; a second rope operates the pulley.

A block and tackle makes it easy to lift heavy support beams and pre-built walls.

Safe Design Checklist

Safe Design Checklist

- ❏ Platform no more than 8 ft. above ground (for kids' treehouse).
- ❏ Strong railings 36" high, with balusters no more than 4" apart.
- ❏ Continuous railing along all open decks and at sides of stairs.
- ❏ Safety rail across all access openings.
- ❏ No horizontal railing balusters.
- ❏ Large access landings with handles or handholds as needed.
- ❏ No ladder rungs nailed to tree (see page 41).
- ❏ Non-slip decking around access openings.
- ❏ No glass windows in kids' treehouses.
- ❏ Doors and operable windows open onto a deck, not a drop.
- ❏ Soft ground cover beneath kids' treehouses.
- ❏ Hardware countersunk in all exposed areas.
- ❏ No rough wood edges, sharp points, or protruding nails or screws.
- ❏ Screws and bolts only for structural connections to tree; no nails (see page 46).
- ❏ Regular maintenance check of platform support members and tree connections, railings, access equipment, and handles.

Safe Construction Checklist

- ❏ Safety ropes and harness for any high work.
- ❏ Tie onto safety line even after platform is complete.
- ❏ No kids or visitors under tree during construction.
- ❏ Hardhats for workers on ground and all kids.
- ❏ Follow basic construction safety and ladder safety rules.
- ❏ No beer before quittin' time.

Treehouse Techniques

uilding a treehouse is mostly an exercise in carpentry. But even if you have years of experience pounding nails and planing doors with your feet firmly on the ground, you'll find that everything changes once you're up in the air. The simplest tasks take on new challenges as you struggle to keep the counterforces of work from knocking you to the ground. But in the end, whether you're building a treehouse or an outhouse or a doghouse, the success of the project comes down to good design and sound techniques. We've discussed good design already. Now it's time to take a look at treehouse building techniques.

Building Platforms

t's time to get this house off the ground. The platform is the first and most important part of the building process. It also tends to be the most challenging, so unfortunately there's no warming up on the easy stuff. Do a good job here and for the rest of the project you'll have the satisfaction of knowing your house will be safe, secure, and, hopefully, level.

To build a proper platform, you'll need to determine what types of anchors will hold up best against the host tree's natural movement throughout the year. You'll also decide on sizing for support beams and floor framing, based on the size of your house and how much it will weigh (don't worry, you won't have to stand on a scale with each 2 × 4).

As before, the tree should be your primary guide.

This chapter walks you through some basics of platform construction, the main types of anchors for support beams, and installation of the floor decking. You'll then get a construction overview of platforms for several popular treehouse configurations. Please keep in mind that all methods and configurations shown here are merely drawn from examples that have worked on other treehouses. On your own treehouse, you alone are the architect, engineer, and builder, and it's up to you to determine what is suitable for your situation. If you have any concerns about the structural viability of your platform or the health of your tree, consult a qualified building professional or arborist.

The treehouse platform needs to be solidly constructed, square, level and (above all) securely attached to the tree or trees.

Platform Basics

A typical treehouse platform is made up of support beams and a floor frame. The beams are anchored to the tree and carry the weight of the entire structure. The frame is made up of floor joists that run perpendicular to the beams. Topped with decking, the floor frame becomes the finished floor of the treehouse, onto which you build the walls and everything thereafter. Some small kids' treehouses have only a floor as the supporting structure, particularly when the house is low to the ground and is well supported by branches.

Sizing beams and floor joists isn't an exact science, as it is more or less with a regular house, but standard span tables can give you an idea about load limits for your treehouse. Contact your local building department for span tables and materials requirements for beams (also called girders), floor joists, and decking materials. What's unique to treehouses is the additional stress of the tree's motion and possible twisting forces applied to the floor frame. Flexible anchors are the best defense against tree motion, as you'll see later. In any case, it's better to err on the side of oversizing support members.

The trick to building a successful platform is not just in the strength and stability. The platform must also be level. If you've ever been in an old house with a sloping floor, you know why. It messes with your sense of equilibrium and gives you an uneasy "funhouse" feeling. In a treehouse this can lead to a per-

ceived sense of instability, plus it gives your friends and family something to make fun of. One handy technique for locating anchor points to create a level platform is to set up a mason's string and line level. A few more tips for building platforms:

- Use a single ¾"-dia. galvanized lag screw to anchor lumber directly to the tree. For lightweight supports, you can get away with ½" screws, but don't use anything smaller.
- If a situation calls for more than one screw in any part of the tree, never place two screws in a vertical line less than 12" apart. To the tree, each screw is treated as a wound; if the screws are too close together, the wounds might coalesce, causing the area to rot.
- Never remove bark to create a flat surface for anchoring, etc. If done carefully, it's okay to shave the surface slightly, but always leave the protective layer of bark intact. A better solution is to use wood wedges to level out brackets and other anchors.
- When you're building a platform up in the tree, it's often helpful to cut beams or joists long at first, allowing some play as you piece the frame together. Cut off the excess after the framing is completed, or leave beam ends long to use as outriggers for pulleys, swings, etc.

Fasteners placed close together in a vertical line can lead to rot in the tree, causing the anchors to fail.

Platform Anchoring Techniques

Anchoring the platform is all about dealing with tree movement. Here's the problem: If you're building in or around a section of the tree that's used to moving a lot in the wind, and you tie multiple parts of the tree (or parts of different trees) together, something's got to give. Usually it's your platform's support beams or anchors that lose the battle by breaking or simply shearing off. The best solution is to respect Mother Nature by using anchors that make allowances for movement.

Treehouse builders have come up with a range of anchoring methods for different situations, but most fall into one of the four categories shown here. Knowing the main types of anchors will help you decide what's best for your project. Often a combination of different anchors is the most effective approach.

Fixed Anchor

A fixed anchor is the most basic type, with the support beams firmly anchored to the tree with large lag screws. Because they allow for zero tree movement, fixed anchors are typically used on single-tree houses anchored exclusively to the trunk, or perhaps used in conjunction with a flexible anchor (sliding or hanging—see below) at the opposite end of the beam.

To install a fixed anchor, drill a slightly oversized hole for a lag screw through the beam, just below the center of the beam's depth. Drill a pilot hole into the tree that's slightly smaller than the screw's shank. Add one washer on the outside of the beam and one or two large, thick washers on the tree side, and anchor the beam to the tree with the lag screw. The washers on the tree side of the beam help prevent chafing of the beam against the bark.

Sizing the screw: Use a ¾" galvanized lag screw that's long enough to penetrate at least 5" to 6" into the tree's solid wood. Accounting for a 2× (1½"-thick) beam, the washers, and the bark, you need at least a 9" screw for a major beam connection.

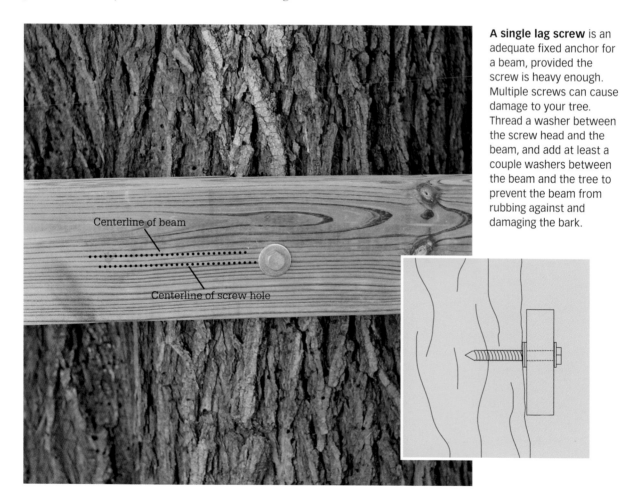

Centerline of beam

Centerline of screw hole

A single lag screw is an adequate fixed anchor for a beam, provided the screw is heavy enough. Multiple screws can cause damage to your tree. Thread a washer between the screw head and the beam, and add at least a couple washers between the beam and the tree to prevent the beam from rubbing against and damaging the bark.

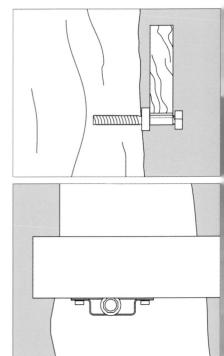

A slot-type sliding anchor allows single-directional movement between the tree or trees and the platform beams.

A bracket-type sliding anchor allows two-directional movement while offering solid support. Unfortunately, you'll have to have these custom-fabricated at a local metal shop.

A specialty treehouse anchor offers the best combination of strength and movement allowance. The Garnier Limb anchor illustrated here is very popular with professional treehouse builders and can be purchased on the Internet (see Resources).

Sliding Anchor

There are two main types of sliding anchor: slot-type and bracket-type. The slot-type is a simple variation of the fixed anchor, but instead of a drilling a hole in the beam for the lag screw, you cut a slot that allows for a few inches of lateral movement. This anchor is suitable for relatively small, low treehouses that don't warrant the heavy-duty support of a bracket-type connection. Using a ¾" lag screw and extra-large washers on both sides of the beam, make the slot 1" wide and 3" to 6" long. Leave the screw slightly loose to allow a little play for the beam to slide.

A bracket-type sliding anchor uses a metal bracket or cleat mounted to the tree to support the beam from below. As the tree moves, the beam is free to slide along the top of the support without rubbing against the tree. A properly engineered and installed bracket makes a very strong anchor suitable for large treehouses.

Unfortunately, they don't sell treehouse brackets at your local hardware store. So how do you get them? One way is to have them custom built to your specifications by a qualified welder. Another option is to use a Garnier Limb, or "GL," a manufactured metal anchor specifically designed for supporting treehouse beams. The GL has a threaded screw end that screws into the tree and a smooth "limb" end that supports the beam.

The developers of the GL have come up with many variations based on their basic anchor to accommodate various treehouse configurations. You can see the GL in action and get ordering and installation information on their website: www.treehouses.com. According to the website, the basic installation of a Garnier Limb has a load rating of 4,000 pounds.

Hanging Anchor

With a hanging anchor, the beams are actually suspended from the tree by cables or moveable hardware, making it the most flexible type of joint. This flexibility makes it ideal for difficult applications, such as when tree movement is significant or when the branch or trunk configuration won't easily accommodate a platform. Note: The minimum branch size for hanging anchors (at the connection point) is 6" dia., depending on the tree and treehouse.

As with the sliding anchor, there are different styles of hanging connections. A basic cable setup offers the best flexibility: Cut a 6-ft. length of heavy-duty rust-proof cable, then cut enough high-tensile rust-proof chain to wrap around the beam twice, plus a few extra links. Drive a ⅝" eye lag screw into the tree, about 4 ft. above the desired beam elevation. Position the eye screw so its shaft will be perpendicular to the cable when hung. This ensures that the load will rely more on the screw's shear strength than the grip of the threads.

Hang the beam in the tree at the desired elevation, using temporary lines. Thread the cable through the eye screw, using a cable thimble to protect the cable, then secure the end with three cable clamps. Wrap the beam with the chain and secure the ends to the cable, again using a thimble and three clamps. To prevent the beam from slipping out of the anchor, make sure plenty of beam extends past the chain, and install a strong metal bracket that loosely captures the chain at the bottom edge of the beam.

Another type of hanging anchor uses a long, ⅝" eye through bolt that extends completely through a support branch. At the other end, another eye bolt extends through the beam and is secured below. The two eyes are connected with a heavy-duty shackle, allowing some movement in all directions.

Bolting through the branch won't hurt the tree, but the branch must be at least 6" in diameter for this application. Make sure to use a strong washer on the top side of the branch, as well as a washer or steel bearing plate below the beam. If you use a built-up beam (with two 2× boards nailed together), add pairs of carriage bolts along both sides of the eye bolt, to keep the beam members together when the anchor is under stress.

With any type of hanging anchor, it's important that the beam and cable or hardware do not rub against the tree. If your setup doesn't allow for at least 6" of play between the beam/hanger and the tree, fasten a wood block to the tree to protect against chafing that could damage the bark and underlying layers. Also, never hang a support cable or chain by running it over a branch or wrapping it around a branch or trunk. This can kill part or all of the tree.

A screw eye or through bolt hanging anchor requires a tree limb at least 6" in diameter.

A hanging anchor with cable attaches to a screw eye in the tree and a doubled ¾" chain wrapped around the beam.

Knee braces support the platform, distributing the load onto the trunk and off of the lag screws that attach the beams to the tree trunk.

Knee Braces

Knee braces help support many types of platforms after the main beams have been attached to the tree. As such, they might be considered secondary anchors but nevertheless are critical to many platform designs.

A knee brace essentially is an angled strut that forms a structural triangle with the platform and the tree. It is strongest when set at 45° (or as close as possible to that angle). There are numerous designs of braces for treehouses, but all follow the same principle of the triangle.

For strength, the top end of the brace should meet the beam or frame at least ⅔ of its total distance from the tree. Don't worry if the braces aren't all same length; it's more important to maintain the 45° angle. To join the top end of the brace to the corner of a platform frame, use adjustable framing connectors. To anchor to the underside of a beam or joist, use pairs of metal joining plates, bolted to both members with carriage bolts.

Attaching the brace to the tree is another matter. Large, professionally built (yes, there are people who get to do this for a living) treehouses often use custom metal brackets to affix knee braces to the tree. An easy amateur method is to use a adjustable framing connector screwed to the tree and fastened to the brace with nails.

Installing Decking

If you're thinking that you've just jumped from platform beams to decking and skipped the floor framing, you're right. Because the configuration of the floor framing tends to follow the platform design, you'll get a better picture of that with the individual construction overviews starting on page 67.

Most treehouse platforms are decked using standard decking techniques. It's a lot like decking a... well, a deck, or a floor, depending on the materials used. Standard decking materials include 5⁄4 × 6 decking boards, 2 × 6 lumber, and 3⁄4" exterior-grade plywood. Of these, plywood is the cheapest and easiest to install, but it comes with one drawback: Treehouse floors tend to get wet, and the water has no place to go on a solid plywood surface. By contrast, decking boards can—and should—be gapped to allow water through and eliminate pooling. If you're really committed to creating a dry interior on your house, you might

consider plywood or tongue & groove decking boards, which make a smooth, strong floor without gaps.

Install decking boards with deck screws driven through pilot holes (although you would normally nail tongue & groove boards). Use screws that are long enough to penetrate the floor framing by at least 1 1⁄4". Gap the boards 1⁄4" apart, or more, if desired. Two screws at each joist are sufficient. Install plywood decking with 2" deck screws, driven every 6" along the perimeter and every 8" in the field of the sheet.

To allow for tree growth, try to leave a 2" gap between the decking and the tree. This means you'll have to scribe the decking and cut it to fit around tree penetrations. To scribe a board, set it on the floor as close as possible to its final position, then use a compass to trace the contours of the tree onto the board.

2" gap

Fasten the decking to the floor frame with corrosion-resistant deck screws. INSET: Use a compass to scribe decking boards at tree penetrations.

A single-tree treehouse often is constructed so the tree penetrates the platform more or less in the middle. The platform is supported by beams that are lag-screwed to the tree. This platform will be reinforced with knee braces.

Platform Designs

Following are five examples of platforms in different tree configurations, along with construction overviews for building the platforms as shown. Hopefully they will help you generate ideas for building your own platform.

These examples are for demonstration purposes only. The proper sizing of support beams, joists, and hardware, as well as platform configuration, must be based on your tree and house project.

Single Tree: Platform Nestled in Branches

This is a simple platform design suitable for a small kids' treehouse. Because the platform is small (about 5 × 6 ft.) and has support from several branches, there are no support beams. Instead, a sturdy floor frame made with 2 × 6s is anchored directly to the tree. To account for slight branch movement, two of the four anchors are slot-type sliding connections and two are fixed anchors. The floor decking is ¾" plywood. For this type of platform, the support branches should be at least 6" in diameter.

Finding the Anchor Points

Using four nails and a mason's string, plot the rough platform shape onto the support branches. Attach a line level to the string, and work your way around the four sides, adjusting the nails up or down as needed to create a level layout. Each nail represents an anchor point, as well as the approximate center of the floor frame members. When you're satisfied with the layout, remove the string, but leave the nails in place to help with measuring and positioning the frame members.

Installing the Rim Joists

Using the nails for reference, measure the approximate length of the first rim joist. Cut the joist long by about 12" to allow for some play when positioning the two perpendicular rim joists. Mark the locations of the two fixed anchor points onto the board, then drill a through hole for a ¾" lag screw, a little below the center of the board's depth (see page 61). Reposition the

joist in the tree, then check it for level. Drill a ⅝"-dia. pilot hole into the tree at one of the anchor points. Add washers to both sides of the joist, and fasten the joist with a lag screw. Holding the joist level, drill a pilot hole and install the second fixed anchor.

TIP: If the joist won't install plumb because the branch is not vertical, glue a wood wedge behind the joist with construction adhesive.

Cut the two rim joists that run perpendicular to the first rim joist. Have a helper hold one end while you level and mark the anchor point on the other end. Cut a 1" × 3" to 1" × 6" slot for the sliding anchor, and fasten the joist to the tree with a lag screw and washers (see page 62). Then, endnail the joists together with 16d galvanized common nails. Install the opposing joist and fasten it to the first rim joist. Cut the fourth rim joist to fit and fasten it with endnails. Cut off the long ends of the first rim joist so they're flush with the mating joists.

Adding the Common Joists

Mark the common joist layout onto the two long rim joists so they will run parallel to the short sides of the frame. Space the joists at 16" or 24" on center; either spacing is strong enough for a small treehouse. Cut the 2 × 6 joists to fit and install them with three 16d galvanized nails at each end.

Installing the Decking

Cut the ¾" exterior-grade plywood decking to fit so any seams fall on the center of a common joist. Fasten the decking to the joists with 2" deck screws.

Anchor one end of the rim joist, then level the joist and anchor the other end. INSET: Glue a custom-cut wedge between the joist and the tree.

Cut the common joists to fit and tack them in place with deck screws so the tops are level. Then drive three 16d nails at each joint (nails have much greater shear strength than screws).

Single Tree: Trunk as Center Post

A tall, straight trunk is the foundation for this platform design that measures 8 ft. square. It starts with two intersecting sets of 2 × 8 beams stacked on top of each other. All beams are fastened to the tree with a single fixed anchor screw. The upper two beams become floor joists in the finished frame. Each corner of the frame is supported by a knee brace, transferring much of the load back down to the tree trunk. The braces are fastened to the frame and tree with galvanized metal framing connectors. The decking is ⁵⁄₄ × 6 boards, which saves a little on weight compared to 2 × 6 decking. The tree for this type of platform should measure at least 5 ft. in circumference at its base.

NOTE: The platform frame is not safe to stand on before the knee braces are installed.

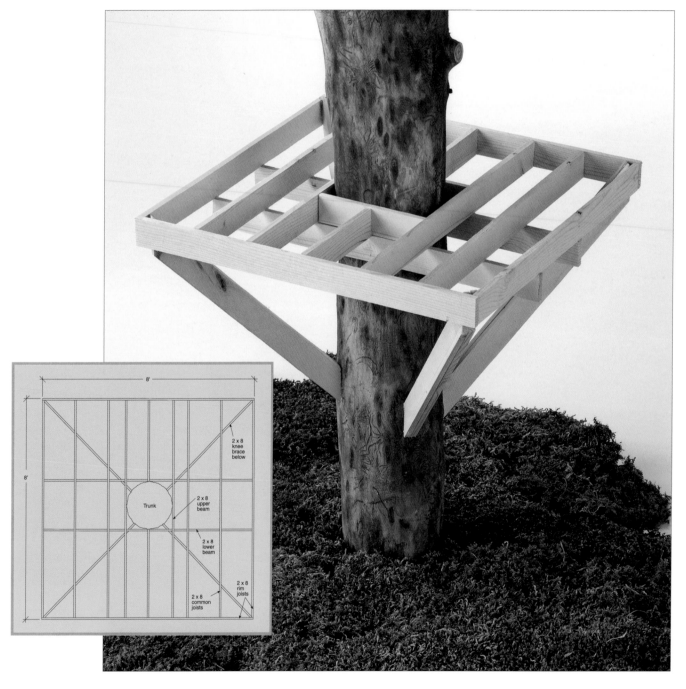

Measure to find locations of platform and bracing, and mark them on the tree with colored tape.

Installing the Beams

Cut the lower 2 × 8 beams at 96", and cut the upper 2 × 8 beams at 93". If possible, find a relatively flat, smooth area of the tree trunk to install the beams. Anchor the first lower beam to the tree with a lag screw, centering the screw along the board's length and on the tree's trunk. Install the second lower beam on the opposite side of the trunk, making sure the two beams are level with each other and are even on the ends. Install the upper beams on top of the lower beams, following the same procedure.

Adding the Rim Joists

Cut two 2 × 8 side rim joists at 96" and two end rim joists at 93". The end joists are parallel to the upper beams. Fasten the side joists over the ends of the end joists, using three 16d common nails at each joint. Check the frame for square, then toenail the rim joists to both sets of beams.

Drill into the tree to make pilot holes for the lag screws. Because you will be driving only one screw per beam, you can thread the screw through a guide hole in the beam with washers on both sides of the beam, and then insert the screw tip into the pilot hole in the tree.

Secure the lower support beam to the tree trunk, using a large socket wrench, checking for level.

Level the second lower support beam of the platform base, making sure it is parallel with the first.

Insert shims into the second upper beam prior to securing the beam, checking for level.

Make sure the beams are level with each other before anchoring them to the trunk.

Installing the Knee Braces

Cut each 2 × 8 knee brace to length so it extends at a 45° angle from one of the inside corners of the rim joist frame to the tree trunk; miter the ends of the braces at 45°. Fasten the braces to the frame with adjustable framing connectors (typically used for rafters), using 10d × 1½" galvanized common nails. Install the connectors to the frame first, then fasten the brace to the connector. At the bottom end of each brace, fasten another framing connector to the tree with two ½" lag screws (you may have to drill a pilot hole trough the connector to accept the screw). Fasten the brace to the connector with 10d nails.

Completing the Floor Frame

Cut two 2 × 6 common joists to fit between the side rim joists and install them midway between the upper beams and the end rim joists. Install two short joists that span from the side rim joists to the trunk. Install these midway between the upper beams.

Decking the Platform

Install the ¾ × 6 decking boards perpendicular to the common joists, keeping the decking flush with the outsides of the floor frame. Gap the boards by ¼" and fasten them to the rim joists, common joists, and upper beams with 2½" deck screws.

Framing connectors make for strong joints at both ends of the knee braces.

Toenail all of the joists to the lower beams with 16d common nails.

Two Trees: Platform Spanning Between Trunks

Two large trees spaced about 6 ft. to 8 ft. apart allow for an open platform with a simple structure. This platform is supported by two 2 × 10 beams attached on both sides of the host trees with fixed anchors. The floor frame cantilevers to the sides of the beams and must be supported at each corner with a 2 × 6 knee brace anchored to the side of the tree. This rigid design is suitable for mature trees (at least 10" in diameter) at a low height where movement is slight. As shown, the platform decking is made of 2 × 6 boards. For thinner decking boards two additional common joists are required to reduce the joist spacing to about 16" on center.

NOTE: The platform frame is not safe to stand on before the knee braces are installed.

Installing the Beams

Cut the two 2 × 10 beams to extend several inches beyond the trees at both ends. Anchor one end of the first beam using a ¾" lag screw and washers. Hold the beam perfectly level, then anchor the other end to the other tree. Install the second beam on the opposite sides of the trees, making sure the beam is level and that both beams are level with each other.

Building the Floor Frame

You can build the entire floor frame on the ground, then install it on top of the beams. Just make sure the frame will fit between the trees before completing the frame. Cut the two 2 × 8 end rim joists at 72" and the two side rim joists at 93". Cut the three 2 × 8 common joists at 69".

Nail the end rim joists over the ends of the side rim joists with three 16d common nails per joint so the joists are flush at their top edges. Space the common joists evenly between the end joists, and fasten them to the side joists with 16d nails.

Center the frame on top of the platform beams. Check the frame for square, then toenail the common joists and end rim joists to the beams.

Installing the Knee Braces

Each 2 × 6 knee brace starts about 3" in from the end of the end rim joist and extends down to the center of the tree trunk at a 45° angle. Cut each brace so its top end is flush with the bottom edge of the rim joist and its bottom end has a plumb cut at 45°. Attach the braces to the rim joists with pairs of galvanized metal jointing plates and carriage bolts (see below). Anchor the bottom end of each brace to the tree with a ¾" lag screw and washers.

Decking the Platform

Cut the 2 × 6 decking boards at 96" to run parallel to the side rim joists. Space the boards ¼" apart, and fasten them to the floor joists with 3" deck screws, keeping all edges flush to the outsides of the floor frame.

Secure the braces to the floor frame with metal plates and carriage bolts. INSET: Anchor the braces to the tree with lag screws.

Install each beam so it is level and both beams are level with each other.

Build the 2 × 8 joist frame on the ground, then lift it up onto the platform beams.

Three Trees: Platform Spanning Between Trunks

With the strength of three large trees and heavy-duty bracket-type anchors, this platform is ready for a large, one-story treehouse. The main supports are three 4 × 12 beams, each anchored to a pair of tree trunks.

The platform floor frame is built with 2 × 10 joists spaced 16" on center. It cantilevers about 18" over the front beam, creating a nice spot for a deck area. For decking, the front third of the platform will be laid with 5⁄4 × 6 decking lumber, while the rear two-thirds will decked with 3⁄4" exterior-grade plywood in the area where the treehouse will sit.

Installing the Brackets & Beams

Cut the 4 × 12 beams to length so they will overhang the mounting brackets by at least 12" at each end. Working on one beam at a time, mark the positions for the brackets onto the tree trunks. Note: If you're installing a Garnier Limb (see page 62), you'll need a specially sized bit available for purchase or rent through the GL supplier. Using the bit, drill a pilot hole into the trunk so that the GL will be perfectly level when installed. Drive the threaded end of the GL into the pilot hole, using a large pipe wrench, until the flange is firmly seated against the tree.

Install the brackets and beams one at a time to make sure each beam is level and all beams are level with one another. With a GL system, install a GL floating bracket at each anchor point, following the manufacturer's instructions. Also install a stopper nut on the end of each GL to prevent the beam from slipping off the GL.

Building the Floor Frame

Cut the two 2 × 10 end rim joists to length so they fit between the two front trees with a few inches of play at each end (108" in this example). Cut the two side rim joists and six common joists at 117". On the end rim joists, mark the layout of the common joists, using 16" on-center spacing. Assemble the rim joist frame on top of the beams, using 16d common nails. Measure the diagonals to make sure the frame is square, then install the common joists.

When the common joists aren't supported by a side beam at the rear of the floor frame, reinforce the joists with joist hangers where they meet the rear end rim joist. Check the frame again for squareness, then toenail all of the joists to the beams with pairs of 16d galvanized nails.

Decking the Platform

Snap a chalkline across the joists to represent the outside edge of the treehouse's wall framing. Install ⁵⁄₄ × 6 decking boards perpendicular to the common joists, starting at the front edge of the floor frame and stopping at the chalk line. Fasten the boards with 2½" deck screws. Install ¾" exterior-grade plywood from the edge of the decking to the rear edge of the floor frame, using 2" deck screws.

Add joist hangers to the longest-spanning joists to strengthen their connection to the rear rim joist.

Two Trees & Two Support Posts

Four trees forming a perfect square or rectangle makes for an easy treehouse foundation, but this just doesn't occur often in nature. The platform design shown here provides the same layout with only two trees, and it takes care of tree movement with a floor frame that slides along the top of a support beam. The two posts are 4×4 or 6×6 timbers buried in the ground, set in concrete and reinforced laterally with knee braces. The posts and 2×10 floor frame create a very rigid structure, while the 4×12 beam has the freedom to move on two sliding anchors (see page 62). Using 2×6 for decking boards helps to strengthen the floor frame. For a moderately sized treehouse, the trees for this platform design should be at least 10" in diameter.

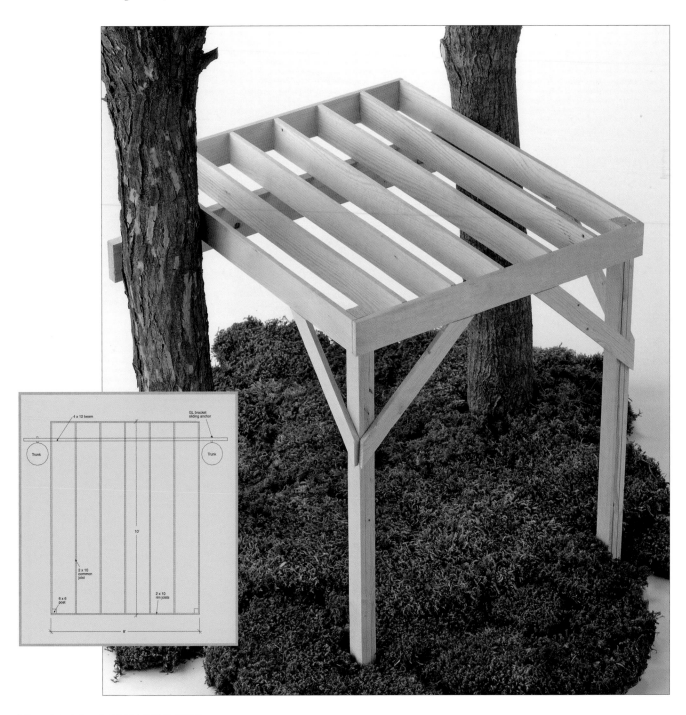

Setting the Posts

Mark the post locations on the ground, allowing for several inches of play between the trees. Dig the post holes 14" in diameter and down to a depth below the frost line (check with the local building department for post-depth requirements in your area), plus 4". Fill the holes with 4" of compactible gravel for drainage.

Cut the posts to length so the tops will reach to the desired platform height when installed. Set the posts in their holes and secure them with temporary cross bracing so they are perfectly plumb and are square to the platform layout. Fill the holes with concrete and let it dry.

Installing the Support Beam

Cut the 4 × 12 beam to extend at least 12" beyond the tree anchor points at each end. Transfer level over from the posts with a mason's string and line level, and mark the post height onto the trees; measure down 9¼" (or the depth of the floor frame, if not 9¼") from these marks to determine the height of the support beam. Install the beam using support hardware at each end.

Building the Floor Frame

Cut the two 2 × 10 end rim joists at 96". Cut the two side rim joists and five common joists at 117". Install the side rim joists and one end rim joist flush with the tops of the post, using pairs of ½" lag screws. Fasten the other end rim joist over the ends of the side joists with 16d common nails. Install the common joists using 16" on-center spacing, fastening them to the end rim joists with joist hangers.

Adding the Knee Braces

Cut the four 2 × 6 knee braces at 48", mitering the ends at 45° to fit flush to the rim joists and post corners, respectively. Fasten the braces to the side/end rim joists using galvanized metal joining plates and carriage bolts. Fasten the bottom ends of the braces to the outsides of the posts with pairs of ½" lag bolts or carriage bolts.

Decking the Platform

Measure the diagonals of the floor frame to make sure it's perfectly square. Install 2 × 6 decking perpendicular to the common joists, using 2½" deck screws. Space the boards ¼" apart.

Brace the posts with cross bracing, then anchor them in place with concrete.

Install the common joists with metal framing connectors (joist hangers), using the manufacturer's recommended fasteners.

Secure the knee braces to the outsides of the posts with ½" lag screws and metal straps.

Once the walls of your treehouse begin to take shape the excitement over your new treehouse will build tremendously.

Walls, Windows & Doors

With the platform done, you're now free to cut loose with your fine carpentry and creative design skills...well, you can use them if you have them. If not, it's ok. The point is, treehouse walls are fun and easy to build, and your new house will start to take shape before you know it. And because much of wall building is relatively lightweight work, it's also a good time to get the kids more involved, for those lucky enough to have some helping hands.

When building a regular house, carpenters frame the walls on the ground, then tip them into place and fasten them to the floor. You can do the same with treehouses, but you don't have to stop with the frame. In most cases, you can add the siding, windows and

doors, and even the exterior trim before sending the whole shebang up into the air. Assemble the completed wall panels with some screws, and presto! you have a house (a topless house, at least; roofs are covered in the next chapter).

Before you get started with the wall framing, plan all the steps of the wall building process—framing, siding, trim, and building windows and doors—to establish the best order of things for your project. If you're using plywood siding, for example, you'll add the siding before the windows, doors, and trim. Other types of siding go on after everything else. In any case, the sequence of information given here should not be interpreted as a specific order to follow.

Framing Walls

In the interest of making friends with gravity, treehouse walls are typically framed with 2 × 2 or 2 × 3 lumber, as opposed to the standard 2 × 4 or 2 × 6 framing used in traditional houses. Single-story treehouses can usually get away with 24" on-center stud spacing instead of the standard 16" spacing. However, the siding you use may determine the spacing, as some siding requires support every 16".

How tall you build the walls is up to you. Standard wall height is 8 ft. Treehouses have no standard, of course, but 6- ft. to 7 ft. gives most people enough headroom while maintaining a more intimate scale appropriate for a hideaway. Another consideration is wall shape. Often two of the four walls follow the shape of the roof, while the two adjacent walls are level across the top. Building wall shapes other than the rectangle or square are discussed later.

Basic Wall Construction

A wall frame has horizontal top and bottom plates fastened over the ends of vertical studs. Where a window is present, a horizontal sill and header are installed between two studs to create a rough opening (door rough openings have only a header, along the top). On treehouses, similar framed openings can be used to frame around large tree penetrations.

In a four-walled structure, two of the walls are known as "through" walls and two are "butt" walls. The only difference is that through walls overlap the ends of the butt walls and are made longer to compensate for the thickness of the butt walls. For simplicity, the two through walls and two butt walls oppose each other so that both members of each type are made the same length.

Build stud walls on the ground and then lift them up onto the platform one wall at a time. INSET: *Through* walls overlap *butt* walls and are fastened together to form a corner of the house.

Through wall

Butt wall

Assemble the wall frame with screws or nails. Add short cripple studs to continue the general stud layout at window and door openings.

To build a wall frame, cut the top and bottom plates to equal the total wall length (not counting the siding and trim). Lay the plates together on the ground—or driveway or garage floor—with their ends even. Mark the stud layout onto the plates, using 16" or 24" on-center spacing. Mark for an extra stud at each side of window and door openings; these are in addition to, and should not interrupt, the general stud layout. If you plan to install interior paneling or other finish, add an extra end stud to each end of the through walls. This gives you something to nail to when the walls are fitted together. Extra studs might also come in handy for nailing exterior siding.

Cut the studs to equal the total wall height minus 3", the combined thickness of the plates. Position the plates over the ends of the studs, and fasten them with two 3" galvanized wood screws or deck screws driven through pilot holes. You can screw through the plates into the ends of the studs, or angle the screws (toenail) through opposing sides of the studs and into the plates. You can also use 10d or 16d galvanized nails instead of screws.

To frame a window opening, measure up from the bottom of the bottom plate, and mark the sill and header heights onto both side studs. Note: If you're using a homemade window, make the rough opening 1½" wider and 2¼" taller than the finished (glazed) window dimensions. This accounts for the window jambs made from ¾"-thick lumber and a sill made from 2 × 4 lumber. If you're using a recycled window sash (without its own frame), make the rough opening 1¾" wider and 2½" taller than the sash. Cut the sill and header and install them between the side studs, making sure the rough opening is perfectly square. Install short cripple studs below the sill and above the header to complete the general stud layout. Follow the same procedure to frame a rough opening for a door, making it 2½" wider and 1¼" taller than the finished door opening (for a homemade door).

Framing Other Wall Shapes

If you're going with a gable or shed roof for your treehouse, frame the two end walls to follow the roof slope. This not only encloses the walls up to the roof, it also establishes the roofline so you have an easy starting point for framing the roof. Houses with hip roofs have four standard walls—with horizontal top plates. Curved walls (for conical roofs) are also flat across the top but are framed a little differently than standard walls.

To frame an end wall for a gable or shed roof: First determine the roof's slope. In builders' parlance, roof slope, or pitch, is expressed in a rise-run ratio. For example, a 6-in-12 roof rises 6" for every 12" of horizontal run, equivalent to an angle of about 26.5°. A 12-in-12 roof slopes at 45°. For most do-it-yourselfers, it's easier to determine the roof slope using only the angle. Another trick to simplify roof framing is to lay out the entire outline of the wall by snapping chalk lines onto a garage floor or mat of plywood sheets. Then you can simply measure to your lines to find the lengths of the pieces.

For a gable end wall, let's say the roof slope is 30° (that's a little flatter than a 7-in-12 pitch). That means the top ends of all the studs, as well as the top ends of the two top plates, are cut at 30°. Snap a chalk line to represent the bottom of the wall, then snap two lines perpendicular to the first representing the ends of the wall. Note: The gable end wall must be a through wall. Measure up from the bottom line and mark the side lines at the total wall height; this is equal to the total height of the side (non-sloping) walls.

Now make a center line running up through the middle of the wall layout. Cut one end of each of the two top plates at 30°, leaving the other ends long for now. Set the angled ends of the plates together so they meet on the center line and each plate also intersects one of the top-of-wall marks on a side line. See your wall now? You can trace along the undersides of the top plates, or just leave them in place, then measure up from the bottom line to find the lengths of all the studs—remember to take off 1½" from the stud lengths to account for the bottom plate. Cut the top plates to length so their bottom ends will be flush with the outside faces of the side walls.

To lay out an end wall for a shed roof—let's say at 15°—snap a bottom chalk line and two perpendicular side lines, as with the gable end wall. The end walls for a shed roof must also be through walls. Mark the wall heights onto the side lines. Snap a chalk line between those two marks, and your layout is done. All of the top ends of the studs are cut at 15°.

Shed end wall layout with 15° roof pitch.

Gable end wall layout with 30° roof pitch.

Framing Curved Walls

Structurally, curved walls are essentially the same as standard walls. They have top and bottom plates, studs, and similar rough openings for windows and doors. The main difference, and the trick to making the curve, is in using a double layer of ¾" plywood for each of the plates. Also, the stud spacing is set according to the exterior siding material. Use 2 × 3 or larger studs for framing curved walls.

Lay out curved wall plates using a trammel: a thin, flat board with a pivot nail near one end and two holes for a pencil near the other end. Space the pencil holes to match the width (depth) of the wall's studs. The distances between the pencil holes and the pivot nail determine the inner and outer radii of the curve. Mark the plate outlines onto full or partial sheets of ¾" exterior-grade plywood, and make the cuts with a jig saw. You can piece together the plates as needed to minimize waste.

Space the studs according to the siding you'll use: For plywood, space the studs 2" for every 12" of outside radius on the curve—a 36" radius gets studs every 6". For other types of siding, such as vertical 1 × 4 tongue-&-groove boards, lay out the studs at 24" on center, then install 2× nailers horizontally between the studs along the midpoint of the wall. The nailers must be cut with the same radius as the wall plates.

Use a trammel to mark the cutting lines for curved wall plates, pivoting the trammel from a centerline.

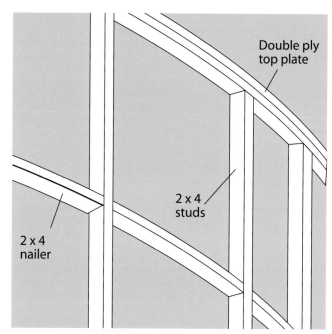

Install 2× nailers between studs for vertical siding. Stagger the nailers up and down to allow room for fastening.

Double ply top plate

2 x 4 studs

2 x 4 nailer

Siding & Trim

Most standard types of house siding are suitable for a treehouse. You might want to match the siding on your regular house or go with something unconventional, such as corrugated metal. Just try to keep the overall weight in check. For that reason, heavy material like hardboard siding isn't a great choice. Three of the most popular types of siding are shown here.

NOTE: Always make sure your wall frame is square before installing siding or trim.

Plywood Siding

Available in a variety of styles, in 4 × 8-ft. panels and thicknesses from ⅜"-⅝", plywood siding is quick and easy to install, and it adds a lot of strength to walls. It is somewhat heavy, though, so you should use the thinnest material that's appropriate. For regular houses, ⅜" plywood siding can be used over studs spaced 16" on center, while ½" or thicker is recommended for 24" stud spacing. On a treehouse, ⅜" is usually fine for either spacing, but it's up to you. Trim goes on after the plywood siding.

Install plywood siding vertically, so the panels meet over the centers of the wall studs. Many types of siding have special edges that overlap at the joints to keep out water; join these according to the manufacturer's instructions. If the panel edges are square, leave a ⅛" gap at the joint, and fill the gaps with caulk after installation. Fasten the panels to the wall framing with galvanized box nails or siding nails. Nail every 6" along the perimeter and every 12" in the field of the panel.

On through walls, wrap the wall ends with a narrow strip of siding. On butt walls, stop the siding flush with the ends of the walls.

Horizontal (Lap) Siding

Classic cedar lap siding is an attractive, lightweight material. It takes more time to install than plywood, and it's more expensive, but it definitely adds charm to a treehouse. Most lap siding requires studs spaced 16" on center. It's easiest to install after the trim. Note: For a large or multi-story treehouse, you might need a base layer of plywood sheathing underneath lap siding, to give the wall sufficient shear strength; consult your local building department or a qualified building professional.

To install lap siding, cut the boards one at a time so they fit snugly between the vertical trim boards. Begin with a starter strip at the bottom of the wall, then work your way up, overlapping each preceding course by at least 1". Nail into each stud with galvanized box nails or siding nails, driving the nails just above the top edge of the siding board below. You may have to add studs near the ends of walls to provide a nailing surface for the ends of the siding.

Install lap siding after the trim is up. INSET: Overlap each course by 1" or more, and nail just above the board below.

Cedar Shingle Siding

Another relatively pricey but very attractive and lightweight option is cedar shingle siding. Tapered cedar shingles are typically sold in 16" and 24" lengths in random widths. They are installed over spaced, or "skip," sheathing: 1 × 2 or 1 × 3 boards fastened horizontally across the wall framing. Like lap siding, each course of cedar shingles overlaps the one below it. The amount of shingle left exposed is called the exposure. The spacing of the skip sheathing should be equal to the exposure.

NOTE: For a large or multi-story treehouse, you might need a base layer of plywood sheathing underneath cedar shingle siding, to give the wall sufficient shear strength; consult your local building department or a qualified building professional.

To install shingle siding, first add the skip sheathing, then the trim, then the siding. Install the skip sheathing over the wall framing with screws, spacing it according to the shingle exposure, which is determined by the length of your shingles: For 16" shingles, use a 6" to 7" exposure; for 24" shingles, a 8" to 11" exposure.

After the trim is up, begin the shingling with a double starter course along the bottom of the wall. Fasten the shingles with 5d siding nails or 1¼" narrow crown staples driven with a pneumatic staple gun. Overlap the vertical joints between shingles by at least 1¼". Install the remaining courses, overlapping each course below to create a uniform exposure. Fasten the shingles 1" to 2" above the exposure line of the succeeding course.

Installing Trim

Simple 1× cedar trim is great for dressing up a treehouse. After the door and window jambs are in place, cut trim pieces to fit along the top and sides of the openings. Miter or butt the boards together at the

Butt together adjacent shingles, overlapping all vertical joints by 1¼" between courses.

corners, and include a ¼" reveal, if desired. Fasten the trim to the framing with galvanized box nails.

Install vertical trim boards at both ends of through walls, wrapping the trim around the end studs so it's flush to the inside face of the wall. You'll most likely have to rip down some of the trim to match the wall dimensions.

Installing Walls

On an ordinary construction job, a wall raising is the day when a few extra helpers show up to tip up the walls and assemble the house frame. With a treehouse, wall raising gets a whole new meaning. It's time to call out your burliest neighbors, or get a little mechanical help from a block and tackle.

To get ready for the wall raising, snap chalk lines on the platform floor to represent the inside edges of the walls' bottom plates. With an accurate chalk line layout, you won't have to worry about squaring the walls as you assemble them.

For a small treehouse with light walls, lift two adjacent walls up onto the platform, set them on their chalk lines, and fasten them together through the end studs with 3"deck screws. Install the remaining walls one at a time, then anchor all of the walls to the platform floor framing with 3½" screws. Drive a few longer screws at floor joist locations.

For larger houses with heavy walls, lay one wall flat on the platform, then tip it up and set it on the chalk line. Anchor the wall's bottom plate to the platform with 3½" screws or 16d galvanized common nails, then add temporary 2 × 4 bracing to keep the wall upright. Hoist up the adjacent wall and fasten the bottom plate, then fasten the two walls together through the end studs. Repeat for the remaining two walls.

When all of the walls are up, cut out the bottom plate at the bottom of the door opening, using a handsaw.

Join the walls with screws driven through the end studs.

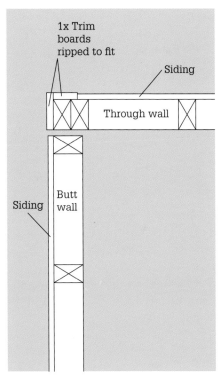

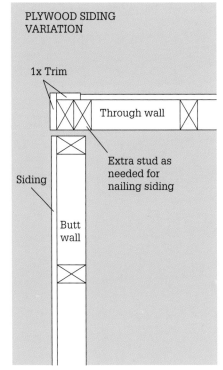

Cut trim boards to fit around the ends of through walls. Butt walls will appear to be trimmed when the walls are assembled.

Making Windows & Doors

Building your own custom doors and windows is extremely satisfying and surprisingly easy. And it's just as easy to build a custom frame for recycled doors and windows. (As we've established, treehouses just aren't the place for fancy store-bought window and door units.) Note for spies, pirates, and other adventurers seeking less conspicuous modes of entry: Trap doors are described in the Accessories chapter (page 104).

Building a Window

It all starts with a simple square frame:
Cut a 2 × 4 sill to equal the span of the window's rough opening, plus 2× the width of the exterior trim. The extra length is used to create "horns" that mate with the bottom ends of the trim on the outside of the wall. Cut a 15° slope into the top face of the sill, leaving a flat portion equal to the thickness of the wall framing. The angled cut should run the full length of the sill. (If you want to get fancy, create a drip edge underneath the sill with an $\frac{1}{8}$"-deep saw cut.) Notch out the horns so the sill fits snugly inside the window opening, and fasten the sill to the rough opening sill with galvanized finish nails.

OPTION: You can use a 2 × 6 to create an extended ledge inside the window.

For the jambs, rip 1× lumber to match the wall thickness. If your framing is 2 × 2, you can use full-width pieces of 1 × 2 for the jambs. Cut the top jamb to span the top of the rough opening, and fasten it to the framing with finish nails. Cut and install the side jambs between the sill and top jamb.

Wrap the inside of the window frame with $\frac{1}{2}$" quarter-round molding, to act as a stop for the glazing. Miter the molding at the corners, and nail it in place so its outside edge is flush with the outside of the window frame. Cut $\frac{1}{4}$" polycarbonate glazing to fit the framed opening and set it against the stops with a bead of clear silicone caulk. Add an inner frame of quarter-round stops, sealed with caulk against the glazing and nailed to the jambs and sill.

If desired, add muntin bars made from $\frac{1}{2}$" strips of wood. Join the bars at the window's center with a half-lap joint (made with opposing notches of equal size), and cope the ends to match the quarter-round window stops.

For a recycled window sash:

Follow the same procedures above, but stop after completing the sill and jambs. Mount the window sash to the side jamb with hinges so the window opens and closes freely. Then, add an outer frame of quarter-round stops snugged up against the closed window. If desired, install a simple hook & eye latch to keep the window closed.

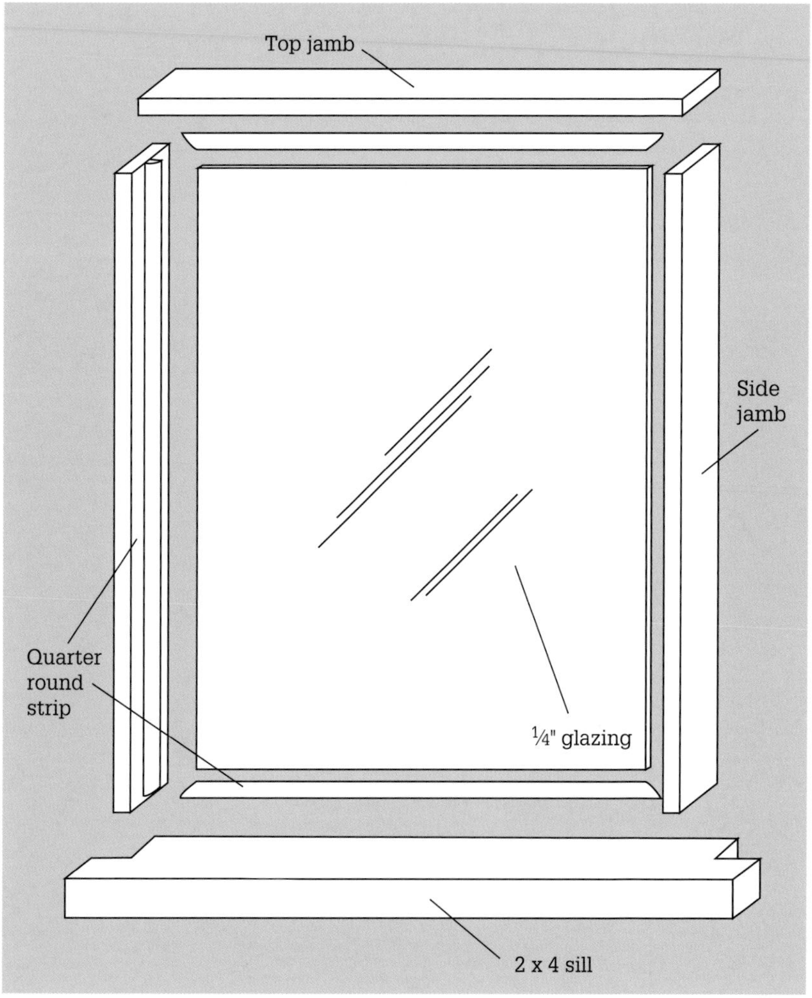

Top jamb

Side jamb

Quarter round strip

$\frac{1}{4}$" glazing

2 x 4 sill

Anatomy of a homemade window.

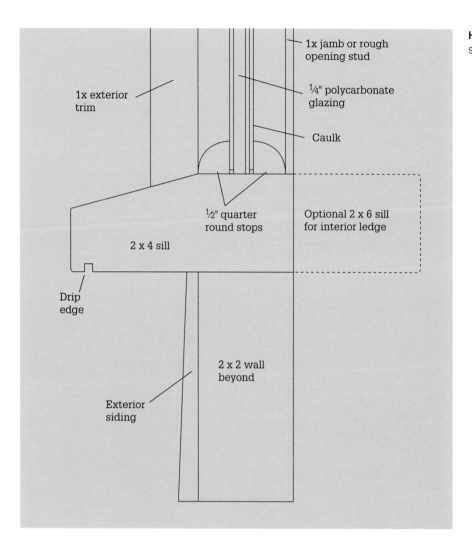

Homemade window: side view detail at sill.

1x jamb or rough opening stud

¼" polycarbonate glazing

Caulk

1x exterior trim

½" quarter round stops

Optional 2 x 6 sill for interior ledge

2 x 4 sill

Drip edge

2 x 2 wall beyond

Exterior siding

Add trim to cover the edges of window and door jambs. Create a reveal by leaving a thin strip of jamb exposed.

Building a Door

As with a window, start with a basic frame: Rip 1× lumber to equal the thickness of the wall frame, plus ¾". Cut the top jamb to span the top of the rough opening. Fasten the jamb to the header with galvanized finish nails so its outside edge is flush with the outside of the rough opening. Cut and install the side jambs to fit snugly between the top jamb and the floor.

Build the door to fit the dimensions of the new frame, leaving an ⅛" or so gap around the perimeter of the door. Be sure to factor in any offset created by the hinges when determining the door dimensions. 1 × 6 tongue & groove boards make great door material: Cut the boards to length and fit them together. Rip one or both side boards as needed to get the desired door width. Cut 1 × 6 Z-bracing to span across the door at the top and bottom hinge locations, then cut an angled piece to fit in between. For strength, the angled piece should point down to the bottom hinge. Assemble the door with screws driven through the Z-bracing and into the tongue & groove boards.

To install the door, first add 1× trim along the inside of the door's rough opening, flush with the room-side edges of the jambs. Mount the door to the jambs using outdoor-type hinges, making sure the door opens and closes freely. Note: As shown here, the door opens in to the treehouse interior. With the door closed, install ½" stops (cut from trim material) along the sides and top of the door. Add a gate latch or other handle to keep the door closed.

You can use the same construction techniques to create a Dutch door. Build two short doors with a slight gap in between, and add a 1 × 4 shelf to the top of the lower door. Hang the door with two separate sets of hinges.

A plain batten door made from 1 × 6 pine has a certain rustic charm. A single Z-brace stiffens the door, but adding a middle rail and second Z-brace prevents warping.

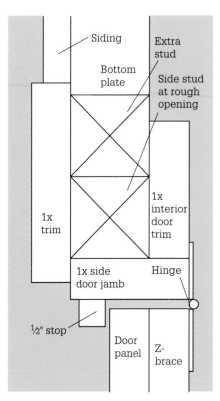

Because DIY doors are not prehung, you'll need to build your own jambs and door stop using the basic configuration above.

A Dutch door has a top and a bottom that open independently (or together if you connect them).

Building Railings

A railing is primarily a safety device. All too often, amateur and even professional designers (especially professional designers) see railings as an opportunity to get creative. The result is an unsuitable railing, which is essentially useless. Build a strong, solid railing with closely spaced balusters and you won't have to worry about who uses the treehouse, whether it's small children or tipsy adults. That means no ropes, no cables, and no twigs. Okay. Lecture over.

A good treehouse railing employs the basic construction details of a standard deck railing. Many treehouse railings are even simpler, eliminating features like the broad horizontal cap rail commonly found on house decks. The important thing is to adhere to the basic design requirements:
- Tops of railings must be at least 36" above the platform surface.
- Balusters (vertical spindles) may be spaced no more than 4" apart.
- Horizontal balusters are unsafe for children, who like to climb them.
- Railing posts (4 × 4 or larger lumber) may be spaced no more than 6 ft. apart and must be anchored to the platform frame, not the decking.
- Top and bottom rails should be installed on the inside faces of railing posts.

- Balusters should be fastened with screws; if nails are used, balusters must be on the inside of horizontal rails.
- All openings in railings—for access to the treehouse platform—must have a safety rail across the top.

To build a simple railing, cut 4 × 4 support posts to extend from the bottom edge (or close to the edge) of the platform's floor joists to 36" above the decking surface. Anchor the posts on the outside of the joists with pairs of ½" carriage bolts with washers. Install post at the ends of railing runs and every 6 ft. in between, and at both sides of access openings and stairways.

Cut 2 × 4 or 2 × 6 horizontal rails to span between the top ends of the posts. Fasten the rails to the inside faces of the posts with pairs of 3" deck screws. Continue the rail through access openings to create a safety barrier. Mark the baluster layout onto the outside faces of the rails, spacing the balusters no more than 4" apart. Cut 2 × 2 balusters to extend from the top of the rail down to the floor framing, overlapping the joists by at least 4". Fasten the balusters to the rails and joists with pairs of 2½" deck screws driven into pilot holes at each end.

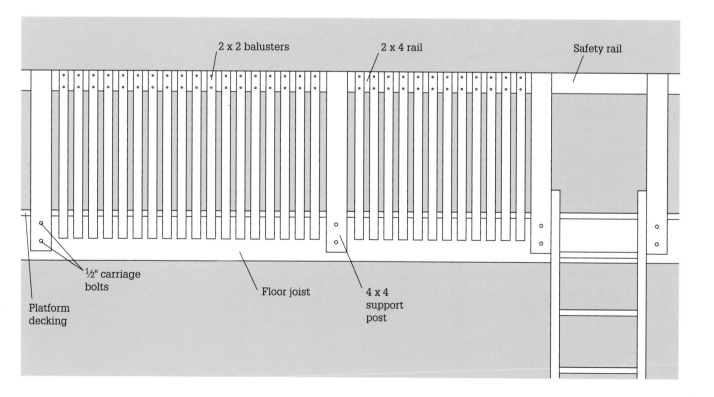

2 x 2 balusters
2 x 4 rail
Safety rail
½" carriage bolts
Floor joist
4 x 4 support post
Platform decking

The structural members that support a treehouse roof generally don't need to be as beefy as the boards used for structures made with traditional building techniques. Here, a 1 × 6 ridge board provides adequate support while keeping the weight of the treehouse down.

Building Roofs

This is it. The home stretch. You're about to become a certified treehouse builder. Or certifiable, depending on how the project has gone. By now your hands are a little callused and your skills honed. That's good, because roof framing usually requires some experimentation and trial-and-error. Oh, yes, and patience.

If you framed your walls with extreme care and everything came out square and perfectly level, you could design your roof frame on paper and use mathematical calculations to find all the angles and locate the necessary cuts. But because you're building in a tree, it can safely be assumed that you improvised

here and there and had to wing it on occasion, or you might not be the type who cares much for calculations. At any rate, most treehouse roof building works best with a cut-to-fit approach.

After the framing is done, you'll sheath the roof and install the roofing material. If the roof is free of intervening tree parts, you stand a good chance of keeping the interior of the house dry. If there are penetrations, you can try to seal them, but you should still find another place to store your signed copy of *Swiss Family Robinson.*

Framing the Roof

The main structural members of any framed roof are the rafters—the lumber ribs that support the sheathing, or roof deck. On a gable roof, the rafters sit on top of the side walls and meet at a ridge board, or ridge beam, at the roof's peak. Rafters on hip roofs also form a peak, meeting at a ridge beam, or more commonly in treehouses, at the tree's trunk. A shed roof has no peak, and the rafters simply span from wall to wall.

A roof's overall strength is determined primarily by the size of rafters and how closely they're spaced. Because treehouses tend to be small buildings, their roofs are typically built with 2 × 3 or 2 × 4 rafters spaced 16" or 24" on center. A small kids' treehouse might be fine with 2 × 2 rafters, while an arboreal palace, with rafter spans over 7 ft., might call for 2 × 6 framing. Snowfall is also a primary consideration in figuring rafter size. If you live in a snowy climate, check with the local building department for rafter span recommendations for your area.

Cutting Rafters

The tricky part to framing any type of roof is figuring out the cuts where the rafters meet the walls and the peak. The cut at the peak is easy in theory: Its angle is equal to the pitch of the roof. If your end wall is built for a 30° roof pitch, the top ends of the rafters for this wall should be cut at 30°. In reality, this cut may need some adjusting, but the theoretical angle is the best starting point.

At the wall-end of the rafter a special cut called a bird's mouth allows the rafter to make level contact with the wall's top plate. The bird's mouth is made with two perpendicular saw cuts. The vertical cut, or heel cut, forms an angle with the bottom edge of the rafter that's equal to 90° minus the roof pitch (in our example: 90° - 30° = 60°). The horizontal cut, or seat cut, is level when the rafter is installed, and meets the bottom edge of the rafter at the same angle as the roof pitch. You don't have to memorize this geometry, but it helps to know the goal when cutting the bird's mouth to fit.

For each type of roof, make some conservative test cuts on a single "pattern" rafter, then adjust the cuts as needed through trial-and-error. When the rafter fits well on your house structure, use the pattern rafter as a template to mark the remaining rafters. If the rafters are tying into an uneven surface, such as a tree part, cut and test-fit the remaining rafters one at a time.

To make a bird's mouth cut, mark the seat and heel cuts, using a rafter square to set the angles (see sidebar on page 96). Cut from one side with a circular saw, then flip the rafter over to complete the cuts, or use a handsaw. Don't overcut the lines to complete the cut, as this can significantly weaken small rafters.

The angles of a bird's mouth cut for a 30° roof pitch.

Cut the bird's mouth with a circular saw, cutting from both sides (or finishing with a handsaw) to avoid overcutting lines.

Framing a Shed Roof

Congratulations. You've chosen the simplest and easiest roof of the lot. You'll be even happier with your choice when it's time to install the roofing. To frame your shed roof, mark the rafter layout onto the wall plates, working from one end wall to the other. For the layout, count the end-wall top plates as rafters; for these, you'll cut special rafters after the others are installed.

Cut a pattern rafter to length so it overhangs the side walls as desired to create a nicely proportioned eave. Set the rafter on the layout marks on top of the two side walls. Mark where both sides of each wall intersect with the rafter (on one side, the rafter won't touch the plate, so you'll have to plane up from the wall with a straightedge). These marks represent the outside ends of the bird's mouth seat cut.

Use a rafter square to mark the bird's mouth cuts. Make the cuts and test-fit the rafter. Adjust the cuts as needed until the joints fit well on both walls, then use the pattern rafter to mark the remaining rafters. Cut the rafters and fasten them to the wall plates with 16d galvanized common nails. At each joint, toenail two nails on one side of the rafter and one nail on the opposite side.

The two special outer rafters go right on top of the end-wall plates. Because they have no bird's mouth cuts, they must be ripped down so they're flush at the top with the other rafters. Use a level or straightedge to plane over from the adjacent rafters and measure down to the top plate to find the required depth for the outer rafters. Rip the outer rafters to size and fasten them to the top plates with 16d nails.

Framing a Gable Roof

The first step to framing a gable roof is preparing the ridge beam. The ridge beam gives you something to nail the rafter ends into and ties them all together for added stability. A 1 × 6 board makes a good ridge beam for 2 × 3 or 2 × 4 rafters. Cut the ridge beam to length so it spans the house between the inside faces of the gable-end walls.

A SQUARE FOR THE HIP ▸

A rafter square (also called a speed square) is a handy tool for marking angled cuts using the degree of the cut or the roof slope. Set the square flange against the board edge and align the Pivot point with the top of the cut. Pivot the square until the board edge is aligned with the desired Degree marking or the rise of the roof slope, indicated in the row of Common numbers. Mark along the right-angle edge of the square.

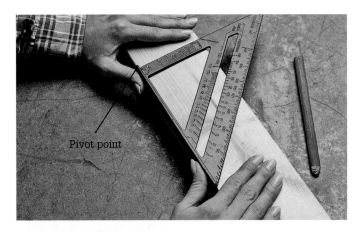

Pivot point

Common markings

Degree markings

Mark the rafter layout onto the ridge beam, working from one end to the other. For the layout, count the end-wall top plates as rafters; for these, you'll cut special rafters after the others are installed. Mark the layout onto both side faces of the beam. Hold the ridge beam next to each wall plate and transfer the layout onto the plate.

From this point, you'll need at least one helper until several of the rafters are installed. Cut two pattern rafters to length so they will overhang the side walls as desired to create a well proportioned eave. Using a scrap cut from the ridge beam, set the rafters on the side walls with the scrap held between their top ends. Mark where both sides of each wall intersect with the rafters (on the inside of the wall the rafter won't touch the plate, so you'll have to plane up from the wall with a straightedge). These marks represent the outside ends of the bird's mouth seat cut.

Use a rafter square to mark the bird's mouth cuts. Make the cuts and test-fit the rafters. Adjust the cuts as needed until the joints fit well on both walls, then use the pattern rafters to mark the remaining rafters. Starting at one end of the house, install two opposing rafters with the ridge beam in between so the top ends of the rafters are flush with the top edge of the beam (you can temporarily tack the other end of the ridge to the far wall to hold it up while you work). Toenail the rafters to the wall plates with two 16d galvanized common nails on one side of the rafter and one nail on the other side. At the top ends, toenail through the rafters and ridge with three 10d nails. Repeat to install the remaining pairs of rafters.

The four special outer rafters install on top of the end-wall plates. They have no bird's mouth cuts, so they must be ripped down so their tops sit flush with the tops of the other rafters. Use a level or straightedge to plane over from the adjacent rafters and measure down to the end-wall top plates to find the required depth of the outer rafters. The outer rafters will meet together at the peak, without the ridge beam in between. Rip the outer rafters to size and fasten them to the top plates with 16d nails.

Test-fit the pattern rafters on the walls, using a scrap piece to act as the ridge beam.

Toenail the rafters to the wall top plates with three nails driven into the plates.

Level over from the inner rafters and measure to find the thickness of the outer rafters.

Install the outer rafters over the end-wall plates so the rafter ends meet at the roof peak.

Framing a Hip Roof

A simple hip roof has the perfect shape for capping off a square treehouse surrounding a central trunk. Since the roof pitch has yet to be determined, first pick an angle that looks good to you—let's say 40°. Cut one end of a pattern rafter at 40°. Use a handsaw or circular saw to bevel the edge of one of the outside wall corners at 40°. This creates a flat surface for receiving the rafter. Set the rafter on the wall and the tree. If everything looks good, mark where the top of the rafter meets the tree. Use a level to extend this mark around the perimeter of the trunk.

Using the pattern rafter, mark the cuts for three more corner rafters (the hip rafters). Cut off the remaining three wall corners to match the first. Install the four hip rafters so their top ends are on the tree marking and their bottom ends rest on the walls. Fasten the rafters to the tree with 3½" galvanized wood screws; fasten to the walls with screws or 16d galvanized common nails. Drive two toenails (or screws) on one side of the rafter and one nail on the other side.

To cut the interior, or common, rafters, set up two mason's lines: one line running between the tops of the hip rafters, directly above where they meet the walls, and one line strung around the ends of the hip rafter tails. Use the lines for reference as you cut the common rafters to fit the structure. Mark the common rafter layout onto the top wall plates, centering a full-length rafter between each pair of hip rafters. You'll probably also need two or more short rafters that run from the hip rafters to the walls. These are called jack rafters.

The commons and jacks get a bird's mouth cut to rest on top of the wall. Cut and test-fit the rafters one at a time, using the strings to help with measurements. Cut the common rafters long to start with, then miter the top ends to fit roughly to the tree, followed by the bird's mouth. To cut the jack rafters, bevel the top ends to fit flush against the side faces of the hip rafters. This can be a difficult cut but doesn't have to be perfect; just get it close enough to make a strong joint. When all joints fit well, cut the bottom end of each rafter to length so it meets the outer mason's line. Fasten the rafters as you fastened the hip rafters.

A clipped corner has part of the siding and cap plate cut away so the hip rafter can sit squarely on top of the wall.

String mason's lines from rafter tip to rafter tip and test with a line level to make sure that the rafters are all level to one another.

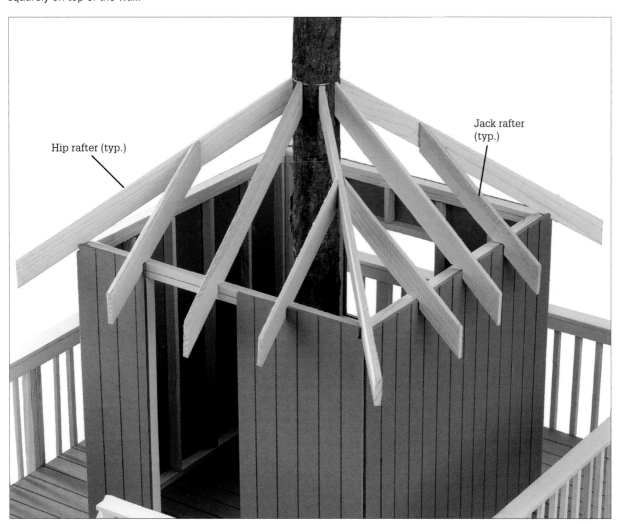

Hip rafter (typ.)

Jack rafter (typ.)

Fasten the top ends of the jack rafters to the sides of the hip rafters.

Sheathing & Roofing

If you've ever built a shed or even a doghouse, you know that roofing a small building can be particularly satisfying. You get to learn and practice basic roofing skills without the backbreaking work of endless roof expanses. The same is true for treehouses.

The first step is choosing a roofing material, and that will determine what you'll use for the roof deck, or sheathing. If you're building a small treehouse, you might want to take the easy route and use a couple of sheets of plywood as the sheathing and the roofing. On any house with a gable or shed roof, consider adding 1× trim up against the underside of the roof sheathing along the end walls, to hide the faces of the outer rafters.

Asphalt Shingles

Asphalt shingles are cheap, durable, and easy to install. They're laid over plywood sheathing and a layer of 15# building paper. They are, however, the heaviest of the standard roofing materials so might not be the best choice if you're trying to minimize weight.

To install an asphalt shingle roof, start with a single layer of ½" exterior-grade plywood sheathing. Working up from the ends of the rafters, fasten the sheathing to the rafters with 8d galvanized box nails, driven every 6" along the edges and every 12" in the field of the sheets. Overhang the rafter sides and ends as desired. Leave extra overhang at the sides of the outer rafters if you plan to install trim there. Cut the plywood as needed so vertical joints between sheets break on the center of a rafter, and stagger the vertical joints between rows.

Add the building paper, overhanging the sheathing along the eave by ⅜". For a hip roof, also overhang the hip ridges by at least 6". Secure the paper to the sheathing with staples. Install the remaining rows, overlapping the row below by at least 2", and overlap any vertical joints by at least 4". On a gable, overlap the roof peak by 6", then install paper on the other side, working up from the eave.

Begin the shingle installation with a starter course: Snap a chalk line 11½" up from the eave (for standard 12"-wide shingles). Cut off ½ (6") of the end tab on the first shingle and position the shingle upside-down so the tabs are on the chalk line. Overhang the side edge (on gable and shed roofs) by ⅜". Fasten the shingle with four 2d roofing nails, about 3½" from the bottom edge. Install the rest of the starter row in the same manner, using full shingles and butting their ends together.

NOTE: For a hip roof, completely shingle one roof section at a time, trimming the shingles along the hip peaks before moving on to the next section.

Install the next course directly on top of the starter course but with the tabs pointing down. Begin with a full shingle to establish a 6" (half-tab) overlap of the tabs between courses. Use four nails for each shingle: one nail ⅝" above each tab and one nail 1" in from both ends. For each successive course, snap a chalk line 17" up from the bottom of the last installed course; this helps you keep the shingles straight and maintains an even 5" exposure. Overhang the first shingle in each course by ½ tab until you get to a 1½-tab overhang, then start over with a full shingle.

To shingle the peaks of gable and hip roofs, cut ridge cap pieces from full shingles, as shown in the photo (at right). Cut one cap for every 5" of ridge. Center the caps over the ridge and fasten them with two nails.

Plywood roof decking is the fastest and usually cheapest type of decking to install. Make sure the plywood you use is rated for use in roofing. If you'll be installing asphalt shingles, a plywood deck is the way to go.

Start installing asphalt three-tab shingles from the eave area of the roof and work your way up toward the peak. If you've never shingled a roof before, make sure to get some experienced help or at least plenty of good information before attempting it.

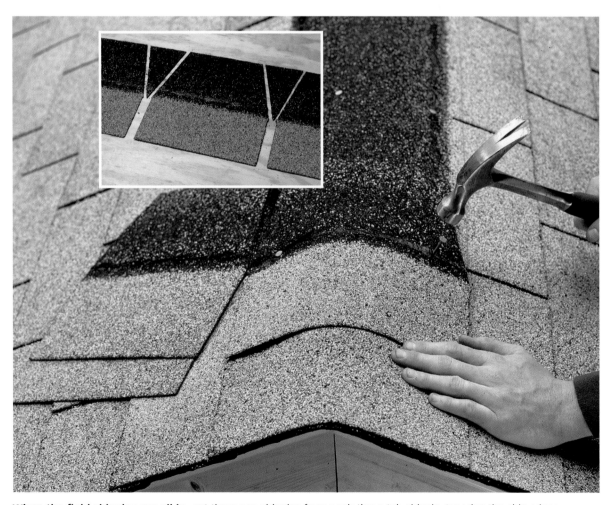

When the field shingles are all in, cut three cap shingles from each three-tab shingle, tapering the side edges slightly as shown. Nail the caps over the ridge so the nails are covered by the next cap.

Cedar roof shingles look terrific up in a tree. Installing them is very similar to installing shingles for siding. Be sure to read the shingle manufacturer's directions carefully to find recommended exposures and installation practices.

(Below) The peak of a roof created with wood shingles will naturally have a seam that needs covering. The easiest way to do this is by beveling two pieces of ridge trim so one piece fits over the other piece.

Cedar Shingles

Installing a cedar shingle roof is almost identical to siding a wall with cedar shingles, which is covered in detail on page 88. The few differences for a roof application are explained here. Note: Don't use cedar shingles on roofs with less than a 3-in-12 pitch (about 14°).

Sheath the roof with 1 × 4 skip sheathing, spacing the boards to equal the shingle exposure—follow the shingle manufacturer's recommended exposure for the size and grade of your shingles and the roof slope. Install a double starter course of shingles along the eave, overhanging the roof edge by 1"-1½" at the eave and 1" at the side. Leave a ¼" gap between adjacent shingles to allow for expansion, and overlap the gaps by at least 1½" between courses.

To complete the peak of a gable roof, layer strips of 15# building paper (tar paper) into the last two courses of shingles, as shown in the photo (above). Cap the peak with custom-beveled 1× trim boards or pre-made ridge caps. Cap the ridges on a hip roof with pre-made ridge caps.

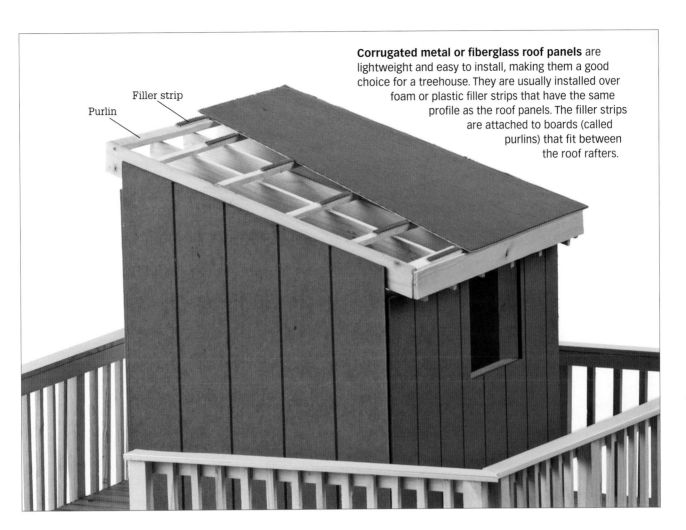

Purlin

Filler strip

Corrugated metal or fiberglass roof panels are lightweight and easy to install, making them a good choice for a treehouse. They are usually installed over foam or plastic filler strips that have the same profile as the roof panels. The filler strips are attached to boards (called purlins) that fit between the roof rafters.

Metal Roofing

With its history as a popular roof material for farm buildings and cabins, corrugated metal roofing has the right character for treehouses. The material usually comes in 2-ft. wide panels in various lengths. Order panels long enough to span each roof section so you won't have to deal with horizontal joints. Installation of metal roofing is specific to the type and manufacturer of the panels you use, and you should follow the manufacturer's instructions carefully.

Here is a general overview to give you an idea of the roofing process: Start by installing 1× or 2× lumber purlins perpendicular to the rafters. Fasten the roofing panels to the purlins with screws or nails fitted with self-sealing rubber washers. Overlap adjacent panels at the ribs, then fasten through both panels to seal the seam. Cap roof ridges with a preformed ridge cap, sealing it to the roofing panels with a sealer strip and caulk.

ROOF, MEET TREE ▶

When roofs leak on regular houses, it's almost always the result of introducing foreign objects—plumbing vents, skylights, dormers, meteorites, you name it. Well, a tree is a very foreign object to a roof, and a large penetrating branch or trunk makes sealing the roof an ongoing challenge. But it can be done. Your best bet is to wrap around the tree and over the top of the penetration with overlapping pieces of neoprene rubber (the stuff used in wetsuits). Seal the

neoprene to the tree with a compatible roofing or gutter sealant. Keep some extra sealant handy for routine spot checks. Clear roof cement, such as the Through the Roof product at right (see Resources) can be used to fill small gaps invisibly. Because it is roof cement, it will remain flexible over time so it doesn't crack.

Accessories

Treehouses are built for fun, and that means there is virtually no end to how you can dress them up. Some of the accessories, such as rope ladders and firepole, have a distinct function. Other accessories, such as zip lines and swings, are mostly about having a good time. Since you won't find any stores called Treehouses 'R Us, you'll have to rely on your imagination, to some extent anyway, to serve as a guide for dressing up your playhouse. But you may be able to find stores that specialize in backyard playhouses and jungle gyms where you can pickup a slide or a disc swing. In the end, however, you're likely to find that the best accessories are the ones you design and build yourself.

Ladders, Trap Doors & Other Modes of Access

Getting from point A to point B can be half the fun of a treehouse. It's one of the things that separates treehouses from other hangouts and play areas. With a little creative thinking, you can devise all kinds of access points and build your own conveyances using standard materials. It's also fun to check out the equipment available through specialty dealers.

So, what's going to be your mode of access? Kids will usually choose the more adventurous routes, like climbing ropes or zip lines. Then again, kids ride bikes with their eyes closed. For you, perhaps a flat-rung ladder is a better choice for balancing ease-of-use and out-of-the-ordinary. Often a combination of travel options is best—maybe a ladder for getting up to the treehouse with an armload of stuff, and a fireman's pole for swashbuckling exits.

A traditional staircase is also an option, and a good idea for anyone with limited agility or for treehouses that receive lots of regular traffic. Building a staircase to a treehouse is a fairly complicated project that's best left to an experienced carpenter. For a pro, the job should take only a couple of days.

The idea of a firepole may fill you with alarm, but kids love them. If you provide supervision and a soft landing place you'll find that a firepole may become the preferred method for exiting (or even entering) a treehouse.

Building Ladders

A handmade, permanently attached wood ladder is perhaps the best all-around means of access for a treehouse. Two good ladder designs are the double-rung and the flat-rung, both of which are suitable for primary means of access. The rope ladder, a kids' favorite, is more difficult to use and serves better as a fun, secondary route.

Double-rung Ladder

This ladder works much like an extension ladder but with greater foot stability offered by the doubled rungs. To build the ladder, start with two long, straight 2 × 6s that are relatively knot-free. These are used for the stringers (side uprights) of the ladder. Set one of the boards on the ground, and lean it against the treehouse platform at an angle that looks comfortable for climbing—60° to 70° is a good range for most situations; we'll use 65° for this example.

Cut the bottom ends of the stringers at 65°. Lean them against the platform at 65° and mark the top ends for cutting. When the ladder is finished, you can fasten the stringers to the platform or to railing posts at either side of the ladder landing. At this point, decide whether the stringers should stop flush with the platform surface or extend above the platform to serve as handholds. Cut the top ends of the stringers, rounding them over or squaring off, as desired. The stringers must be identical in length and shape.

Mark the rung layout onto the front edge of one of the stringers, marking every 10" to 12" and starting at the bottom, front end of the stringer. Standard rung spacing is 12", but 10" is more comfortable for

A double-rung ladder employs pairs of 1½" dowels at each step to create a more stable stepping point. The dowels are glued (with a water-resistant adhesive such as polyurethane glue) into 1"-deep holes in the stringers.

Clamp and glue the doubled rungs as you go. If you space the rung pairs at roughly 12" intervals you should have sufficient flex in the stringers so you can successfully insert each new pair without unclamping the preceding pair.

kids. Make sure the spacing is uniform over the entire layout. Place the stringers together and transfer the rung layout to the unmarked stringer. Extend each layout mark across the inside face of each stringer at 65°, using a rafter square or a template cut at 65°.

Measure in 1¾" in from the front and rear edges of the stringers and mark the rung centers on each layout line. Note: This measurement is for a 1½"-dia. dowel. Cut the rungs to length at 20". This gives you a useable rung width of 18" and a total ladder width of 21". At each rung centerpoint, drill a 1½"-dia. × 1"-deep hole, using a spade bit marked with masking tape to gauge the hole depth. Test-fit several rungs to make sure they fit snugly in the holes.

Lay out all the parts so everything's ready for the glue-up. Working on one stringer, coat the insides of the rung holes with waterproof wood glue; avoid filling up the holes with excess glue, as this will prevent the dowels from setting to full depth. Seat the dowels completely in the holes, using a rubber mallet, if necessary. Make sure each dowel is perpendicular to the stringer. When all dowels are in, glue up the other stringer (it helps to have another person working ahead of you) and set it over the dowel ends, completely seating them in the holes. Clamp the stringers so the ladder is square, and let the glue dry. Secure the completed ladder to the treehouse platform or railing posts with screws.

Fasten the rungs to the stringers, then back up each rung with a pair of 1 × 2 cleats.

Countersink the railing screws so there's nothing protruding above the railing surface.

Flat-rung Ladder

A flat-rung ladder feels a little more like a staircase and is a little easier to climb than a standard ladder. However, for safety, climbers should always face the ladder when going up or down. An optional handrail on each side is a good idea for additional safety. To build a flat-run ladder, follow the steps given for the double-rung ladder (page 106) to establish the ladder angle, cut the 2 × 6 stringers, and mark the rung layout. For the flat-rung ladder, the layout lines for the rungs represent the top of each rung.

Cut 2 × 4 or 2 × 6 rungs to length at 18". This gives you a total ladder width of 21". Fasten each rung with three 3½" galvanized deck screws driven through pilot holes in the outside of each stringer and into the ends of the rungs. Make sure the top of the rung is on the layout line and its back edge is just touching the back edges of the stringers. Reinforce each rung connection with a 1 × 2 cleat. The cleats should extend from just behind the rung's front edge to the rear edge of the stringers. Fasten the cleats with 2" screws driven through pilot holes in the cleats and into the stringers.

To add handrails, cut 3"-long blocks from 2 × 2 lumber, and sand all edges smooth. Install the blocks on the front edges of the stringers at 36" intervals, using pairs of 3½" screws. For the railing, install 1¼" or 1½"-dia. dowel rods or Schedule 40 PVC tubing centered side-to-side on the blocks. Fasten through the railing and into the blocks with 3½" screws driven through counterbored pilot holes. Make sure all screw heads are below the surface of the railing. If you need more than one wood dowel rod for each side of the railing, butt the railing pieces together over the center of a block, and pin the ends together with a couple of angled finish nails to ensure a smooth transition.

Rope Ladders

Rope ladders can be a little tricky to climb, but that's what makes them fun. Kids can pretend that they're scaling up the rigging of a pirate's ship to reach the crow's nest atop the main mast. A handy trick for making a rope ladder more stable is to secure the bottom end to the ground. Once you've hung the ladder, tie the two rope ends together at the bottom with a locking carabiner attached. Clip the carabiner into an eye bolt set in some concrete in the ground. You can easily unclip the carabiner to pull up the ladder into the treehouse.

To make a rope ladder, cut two lengths of ¾" nylon or manila rope, including several extra feet of slack. For the rungs, cut 1 × 4 boards or 1½"-diameter wood dowels at 21". You'll need one rung for every 10" of vertical rise of the ladder. Drill a ¾" hole through each rung, 2" in from each end and centered side-to-side on the rung. Leaving plenty of slack for tying off the rope ends, mark the ropes every 10". Working from the top down, thread each rung onto the ropes and tie a simple knot below the rung so the top of the rung is on the layout lines. Repeat to install the remaining rungs.

Secure the top ends of the ladder ropes to the treehouse's platform framing, railing, or overhead beams using a bowline knot on each rope. If desired, anchor the bottom end of the ladder to the ground, as described above.

Not your everyday ladder. Rope ladders take a little getting used to, but they're a lot of fun. They're easiest and safest to use when they're anchored at the bottom to prevent swaying (you can snap the ladder onto the anchor with a carabiner so it can be pulled up into the treehouse if desired).

Trap Doors

Climbing ropes, secret ladders, and other cool modes of access need an equally cool point of entry: a trap door, of course. The classic trap door is square, with a frame built into the floor joists, and the door itself made from a cutout of the floor boards. Using this basic design you can come up with your own variations—triangular, hexagonal...practically any shape you wish.

To build a trap door, first decide on the size of the opening. With floor joists framed at 24" on center, you're already halfway to making a 22½" square opening. Just add two side pieces between the joists, and the frame is done. With 16" joist spacing, the joists are only 14½" apart—a little too tight for most trap doors. To make a larger opening, cut out the joist running through the planned opening and install two joist headers to carry the cut ends. Then install one or two side pieces between the headers to complete the framed opening. Use the same lumber for the frame as you used for the joists.

Next, add a 1 × 2 stop at each side of the frame, flush with the underside of the floor. Cut out the floor boards flush with the frame pieces (not the stops). Fasten the boards together with 1× cleats or a square of plywood to create the door. Maintain the original spacing between the floor boards so the trap door will blend with the rest of the floor. Mount the door with hinges installed on the back edge of the door so only the barrels of the hinges stick up above the floor. For a handle, cut a finger hole in the door, or install a recessed cabinet pull.

Joist headers support the ends of the cut joist and become two sides of the door opening frame.

A trap door is a fun, secret entry to a treehouse, but it offers some structural advantages as well. For example, if you employ a trap door as your only point of entry you can encircle the treehouse completely with railings.

Fireman's Pole

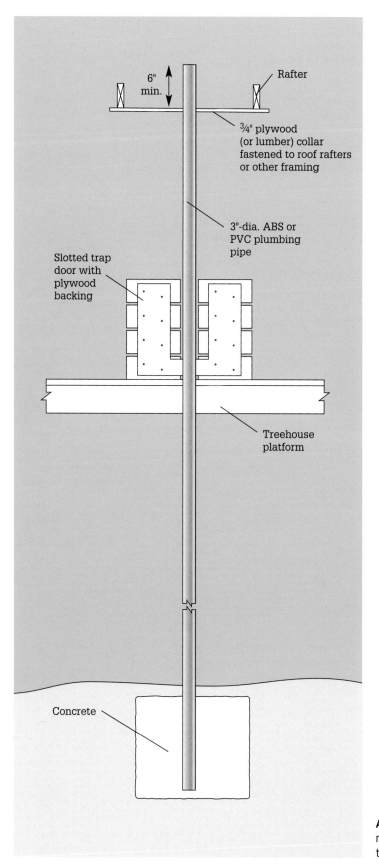

There's nothing better than a fireman's pole for speedy exits. All it takes to build one is a length of plastic pipe, some concrete, and a piece of plywood or lumber. In a firehouse, firefighters zip down a pole through a large, round opening, but you can set yours up through a square trap door—just cut a slot in the door to fit over the pole when closed.

To make a fireman's pole, cut a length of $3\frac{1}{2}$" dia. PVC plumbing pipe to extend from an anchor point on the treehouse down to a foot or so below the ground level. Secure the pole at the top with a $\frac{3}{4}$" plywood or lumber collar with a hole drilled through it that just fits over the pole. Fasten the collar to the roof framing or other support members. With the bottom of the pole on the ground, the top end should extend about 18" above the collar. Position the pole so it's perfectly plumb, then mark where the pole hits the ground. Dig a 12"-diameter × 12"-deep hole centered around the pole mark. Set the pole in the hole and fill the hole with concrete. Check the pole again for plumb and let the concrete dry.

A length of plastic plumbing pipe makes a great fireman's pole. A slotted trap door closes up the access opening.

Image labels

- 6" min.
- Rafter
- ¾" plywood (or lumber) collar fastened to roof rafters or other framing
- 3"-dia. ABS or PVC plumbing pipe
- Slotted trap door with plywood backing
- Treehouse platform
- Concrete

Slides, climbing nets and other fun features add a special element to already-exciting treehouses.

Swings & Playthings

If you came to this chapter first, you're in the right state of mind for owning a treehouse. If you've just finished your treehouse and are wanting to jazz it up a little, congratulations (you're way ahead of the other guy). One thing that most new treehouse owners learn right away is how much their creation becomes a hub of activity. Kids not only play in treehouses, they play under them and around them and, sometimes, when no one's watching, over them. So it makes sense to add a few extra things for kids to do at the treehouse site. And for the adults? This author recommends a hammock. Period.

A few treehouse accessories are easy to make yourself, like climbing ropes and simple swings. Other add-ons are better purchased from reputable retailers. "Reputable" isn't used lightly, either; you don't want a

zip line manufactured from shoddy materials, for example. Since there's no place to shop for treehouse accessories at your local mall, you'll have to be a little resourceful. The best place to start is with an online search under "play structures," "playground equipment," etc, or with keywords for specific items, such as "climbing walls" or "hammocks." A lot of equipment made for play structures can easily be adapted for a treehouse play area.

A reminder about ground covers: While many of us grew up playing on blacktop playgrounds and sports fields that felt like rammed earth, things are different now. Covering a play area with a thick layer of wood chips or other shock-absorbing material is an easy, effective way prevent injury to kids. It's really a no-brainer, as in no one gets brained from a minor fall. See page 53 for more information on ground covers.

Swings & Slides

Treehouses are perfect for swings, slides and other classic playground features. Swings traditionally are hung from trees, and slides need an elevated starting point. Both swings and slides are available in a range of styles from playground equipment suppliers. In addition to the standard favorites, there are now buoy ball swings, tire swings with molded plastic tires (no potentially painful steel belting you get with real tires), and bucket-type swings for toddlers. Slides come in fun shapes like waves, spirals, scoops, and tubes.

A simple disc swing is a good do-it-yourself project with handmade appeal. To make a swing, cut a 10" or 11"-diameter disc from a piece of 2×12 lumber or two pieces of ¾" plywood, making the cut with a jig saw or band saw. If you're using plywood, glue the two pieces together with waterproof wood glue.

Drill a ¾"-diameter hole through the center of the disc. Round over the edges of the disc with a router and roundover bit, then sand everything smooth so there won't be any splinters.

Attach the top end of a ¾" nylon or manila rope to the treehouse or tree, using a ⅝" eye through bolt. Note: Make sure there is plenty of clearance for the swing's travel. The longer the rope, the more clearance is required. Tie the rope to the bolt using a bowline knot. If desired, tie knots at various comfortable heights above the disc location. These give swingers a little extra holding power on the rope. Thread the disc onto the rope and knot the end to secure the disc at a comfortable height above ground. Cut off excess rope and melt or bind the end to prevent unraveling.

Hammocks and swings are natural fits for a treehouse. You'll especially appreciate a swing or hammock that's proportioned to be comfortable for adults, since you'll probably spend plenty of time in it as treehouse play supervisor.

Climbing Features

Kids love to climb. Any parent knows how early in life kids take to climbing—usually inappropriate things like china cabinets—and that this innate drive to ascend doesn't go away. So it makes sense to give kids something safe yet challenging to climb. The newest thing these days is climbing walls.

Climbing walls first appeared in makeshift gyms used by rock climbers to stay in shape during the off season. In recent years, the concept has spread, and today the same basic wall design can be seen in playgrounds, shopping malls, and backyard play structures. You can buy complete manufactured climbing wall panels that mount to a support structure. Or, you can make your own custom wall with plywood and bolt-on handholds available online and elsewhere. The style and arrangement of handholds, as well as the pitch of the wall itself, establish the diffi-culty of the climb. Consult a climbing wall equipment dealer for help with creating a wall that's appropriate for your little monkeys.

One old standby that kids like to challenge themselves with is the climbing rope. You can make your own using a ¾" nylon or manila rope knotted every 12" or so. Anchor the top of the rope to an eye bolt, or just tie the rope around a strong support member on the treehouse. For kids who are too young to have the strength for a climbing rope, a climbing ramp is a good conveyance for accessing a low treehouse.

Another fun skill-builder is the "cargo" net. These are widely available through play equipment dealers. Of course, you want the climbing type of net, not actual cargo netting used for holding down a load in the back of a truck.

Climbing walls seem like a pretty new idea to most adults, but for kids they're practically second nature.

Climbing nets are sometimes called cargo nets incorrectly, but don't confuse the two: they have very different purposes.

Knotted ropes are big fun for climbing and swinging. Look for natural fiber ropes at least 2" in diameter.

Pulleys & Accessories

A treehouse just doesn't seem complete without some kind of pulley hoist. Now that your house is built, you can add a permanent pulley in any convenient location. Choose a suitably strong, corrosion-resistant pulley from your local hardware store or building center. While you're there, buy plenty of rope that's the right size for the pulley, a metal clip or swivel snap, and maybe a 5-gallon plastic bucket or smaller galvanized metal bucket. Anchor the pulley to your treehouse or tree with a lag eye bolt.

The lofty position of a treehouse inspires all sorts of imaginative play. In kids' minds, treehouses become pirate ships, mountainside castles, battlements, spaceships, you name it. There are plenty of toys and props available to reinforce these themes, such as periscopes, ship's wheels, water cannons, and telescopes.

Zip Lines

Zip lines are dangerous. And now that that's out of the way, we can talk about how much fun they are—for the right age of children, of course (and adults). A basic zip line setup includes a tensioned cable strung between two trees and a trolley with rollers inside that glide along the cable. The rider takes off from a raised platform ("Hey, I'll bet that treehouse would make a good platform...") and holds onto the trolley for an exhilarating flight down the cable. Thanks to gravity, the rider dips after the middle of the flight, slows to a stop as the cable rises toward the end of the line, then glides backwards to the low point of the dip, and there makes a safe dismount.

Zip lines are currently available with different types of trolleys, including simple hands-only types and sit-down models with buoy ball or disc seats. Trolleys with seats are safer than hands-only versions because most of the rider's weight is carried by the seat. High-end zip lines include cable tensioners and all kinds of coatings and covers to prevent pinched fingers and other boo-boos. Proper installation of a zip line is critical for safety, as is appropriate riding technique; follow the manufacturer's instructions carefully.

A zip line is strung between two trees with just enough slack that a kid (or adult) can grab onto a trolley device (the handle-and-seat contraption seen here) and take a ride down the line.

Treehouse Plans

No two treehouses are exactly alike because no two trees are the same. But that doesn't mean building plans are worthless when it comes to treehouses. In fact, we've decided to wrap up this book by including six fully developed plans for your consideration and inspiration. It's unlikely that you'll be able to use them exactly as they are shown, so we've left out some dimensions and details that you'll need to fill in yourself based on your tree or trees and on your needs and plans. But we think you'll find them to be a good leaping off point for your venture into the trees.

Plan 1: Gable Roof with Auxiliary Posts

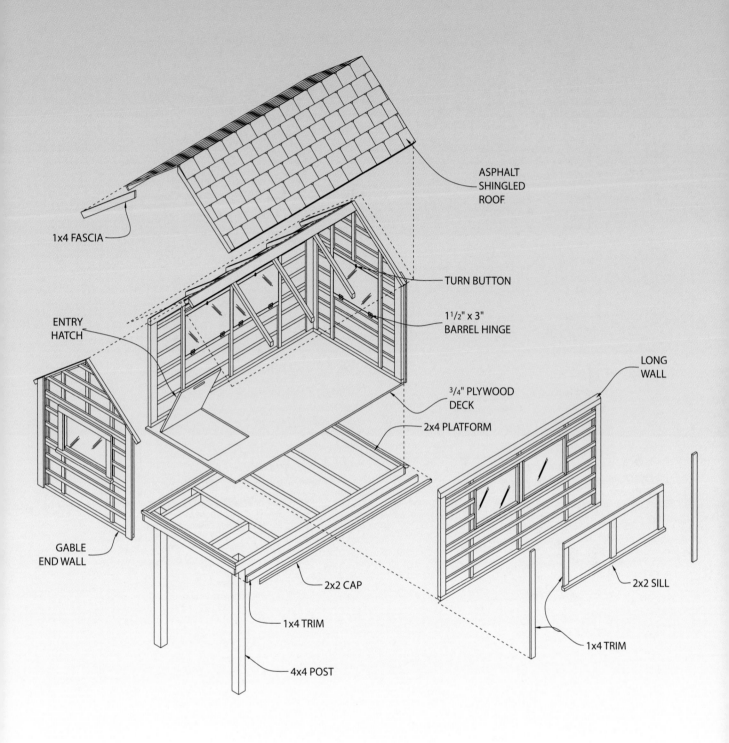

ASPHALT
SHINGLED
ROOF

1x4 FASCIA

TURN BUTTON

ENTRY
HATCH

1¹/₂" x 3"
BARREL HINGE

³/₄" PLYWOOD
DECK

LONG
WALL

2x4 PLATFORM

GABLE
END WALL

2x2 CAP

2x2 SILL

1x4 TRIM

1x4 TRIM

4x4 POST

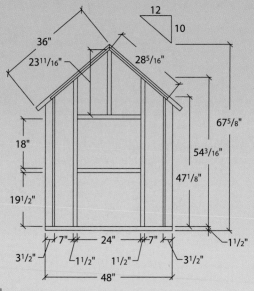

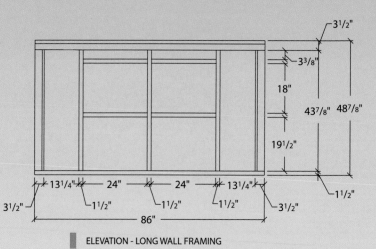

ELEVATION - GABLE END WALL FRAMING

ELEVATION - LONG WALL FRAMING

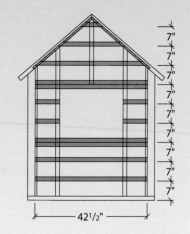

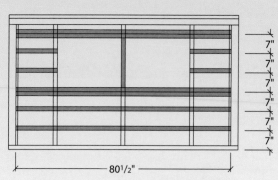

ELEVATION - GABLE END WALL W/SKIP SHEATHING

ELEVATION - LONG WALL W/SKIP SHEATHING

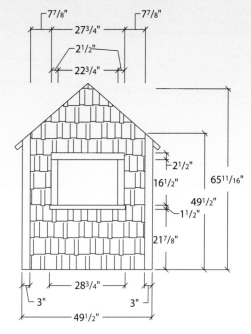

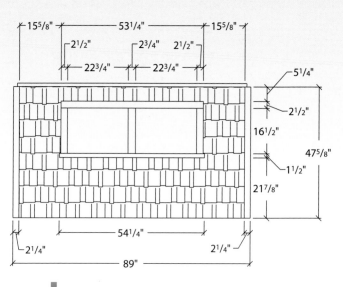

ELEVATION - GABLE END WALL W/TRIM & SHAKES

ELEVATION - LONG WALL W/TRIM & SHAKES

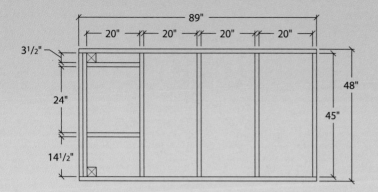

89"

20" | 20" | 20" | 20"

3½"

24"

48"

45"

14½"

PLAN VIEW - PLATFORM FRAMING

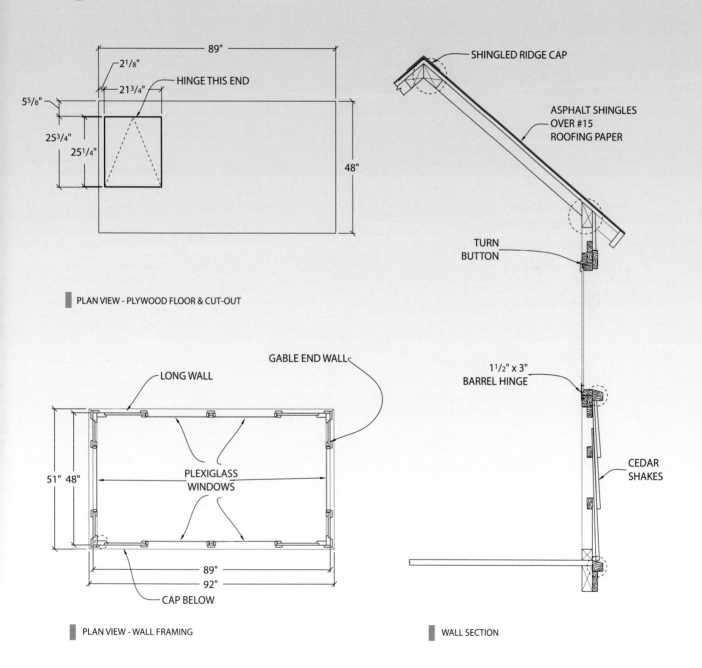

89"

2⅛"

HINGE THIS END

21¾"

5⅝"

25¾"

25¼"

48"

PLAN VIEW - PLYWOOD FLOOR & CUT-OUT

SHINGLED RIDGE CAP

ASPHALT SHINGLES
OVER #15
ROOFING PAPER

TURN
BUTTON

GABLE END WALL

LONG WALL

1½" x 3"
BARREL HINGE

51" 48"

PLEXIGLASS
WINDOWS

CEDAR
SHAKES

89"

92"

CAP BELOW

PLAN VIEW - WALL FRAMING

WALL SECTION

Plan 2: A-Frame with Walkout Deck

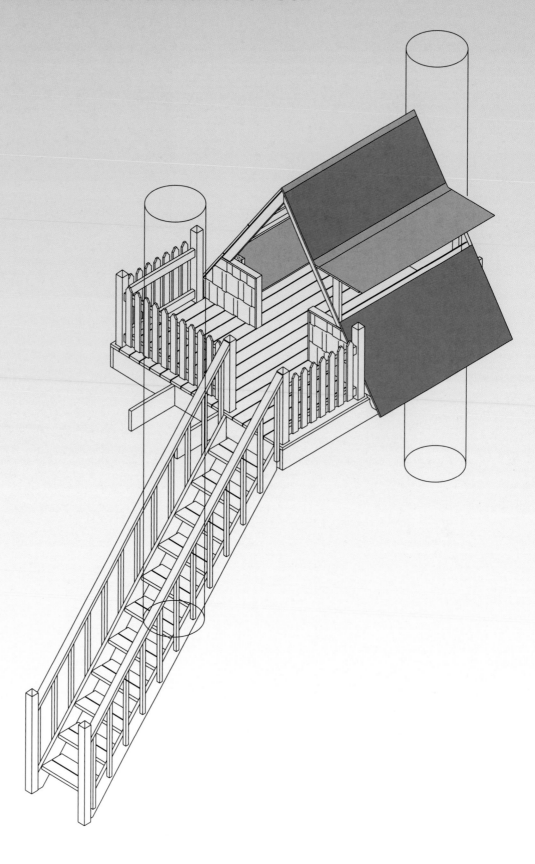

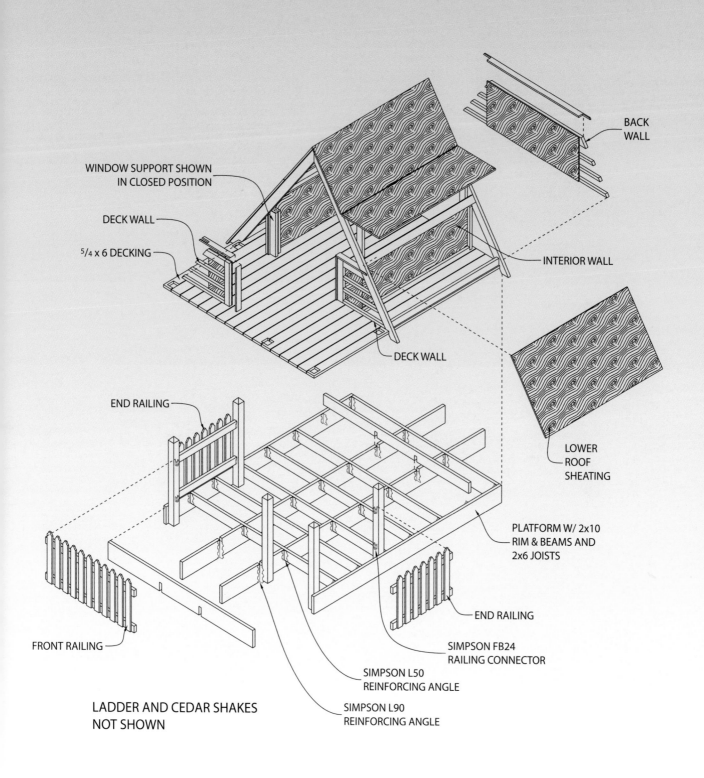

WINDOW SUPPORT SHOWN IN CLOSED POSITION

DECK WALL

⁵/₄ x 6 DECKING

BACK WALL

INTERIOR WALL

DECK WALL

LOWER ROOF SHEATING

END RAILING

PLATFORM W/ 2x10 RIM & BEAMS AND 2x6 JOISTS

END RAILING

SIMPSON FB24 RAILING CONNECTOR

SIMPSON L50 REINFORCING ANGLE

FRONT RAILING

SIMPSON L90 REINFORCING ANGLE

LADDER AND CEDAR SHAKES NOT SHOWN

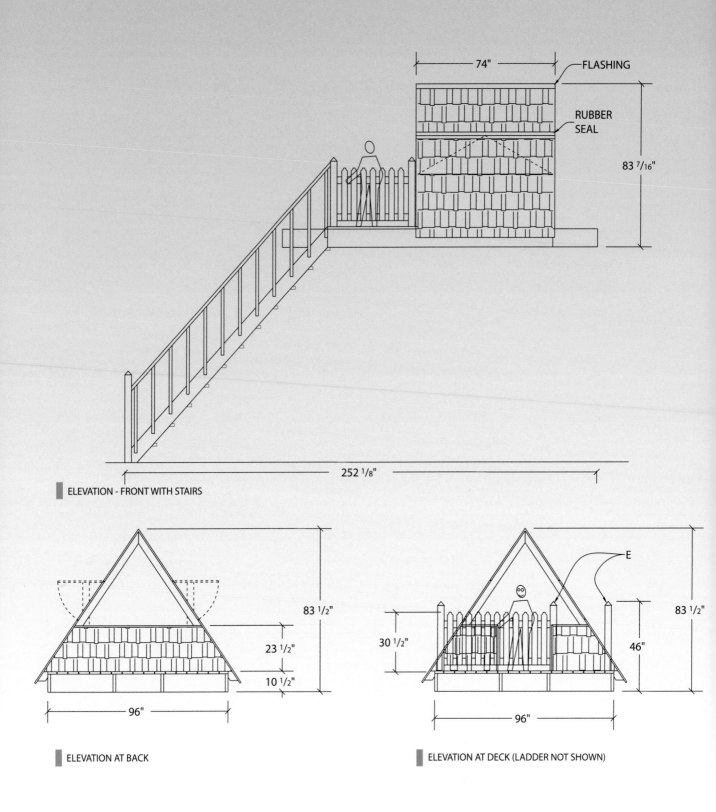

74"

FLASHING

RUBBER SEAL

83 $^{7}/_{16}$"

252 $^{1}/_{8}$"

ELEVATION - FRONT WITH STAIRS

83 $^{1}/_{2}$"

23 $^{1}/_{2}$"

10 $^{1}/_{2}$"

96"

ELEVATION AT BACK

E

83 $^{1}/_{2}$"

30 $^{1}/_{2}$"

46"

96"

ELEVATION AT DECK (LADDER NOT SHOWN)

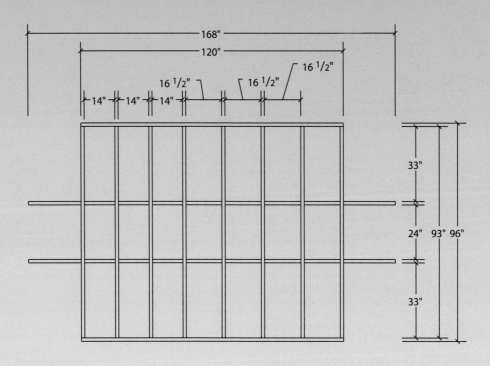

PLAN VIEW - PLATFORM

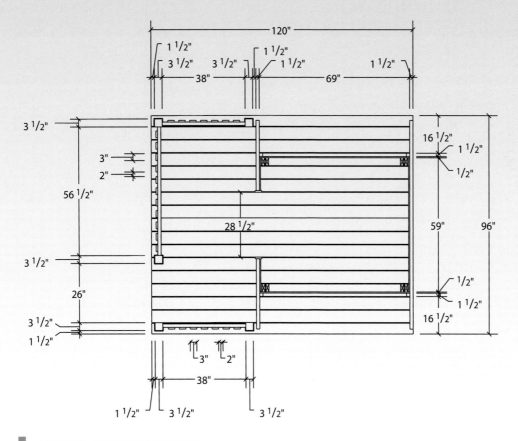

PLAN VIEW - DECK/RAILING/WALLS

Plan 3: Half-covered Crow's Nest

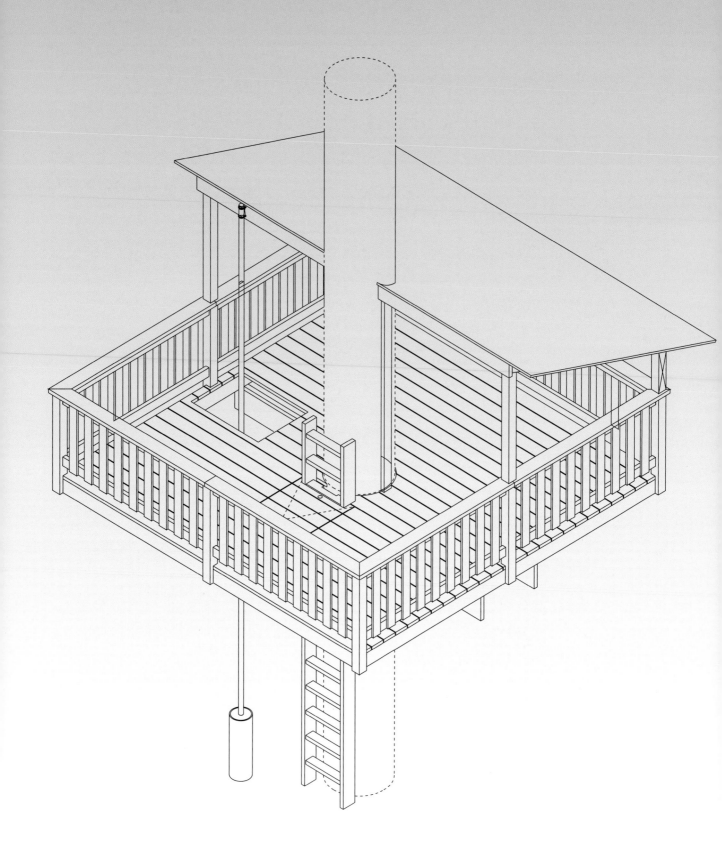

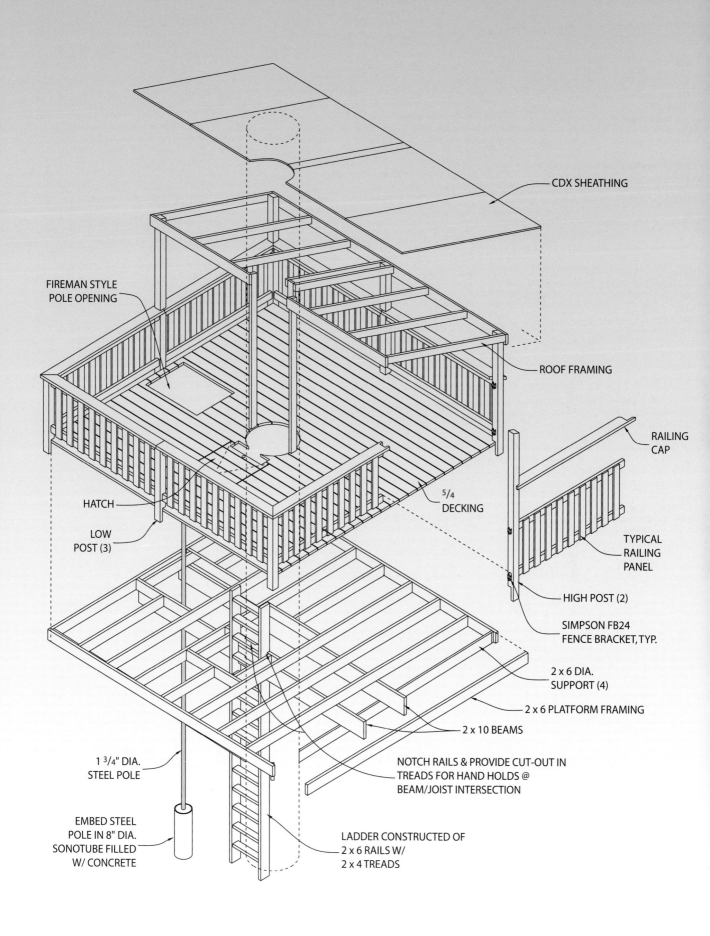

CDX SHEATHING

FIREMAN STYLE
POLE OPENING

ROOF FRAMING

RAILING
CAP

HATCH

LOW
POST (3)

5/4
DECKING

TYPICAL
RAILING
PANEL

HIGH POST (2)

SIMPSON FB24
FENCE BRACKET, TYP.

2 x 6 DIA.
SUPPORT (4)

2 x 6 PLATFORM FRAMING

2 x 10 BEAMS

1 3/4" DIA.
STEEL POLE

NOTCH RAILS & PROVIDE CUT-OUT IN
TREADS FOR HAND HOLDS @
BEAM/JOIST INTERSECTION

EMBED STEEL
POLE IN 8" DIA.
SONOTUBE FILLED
W/ CONCRETE

LADDER CONSTRUCTED OF
2 x 6 RAILS W/
2 x 4 TREADS

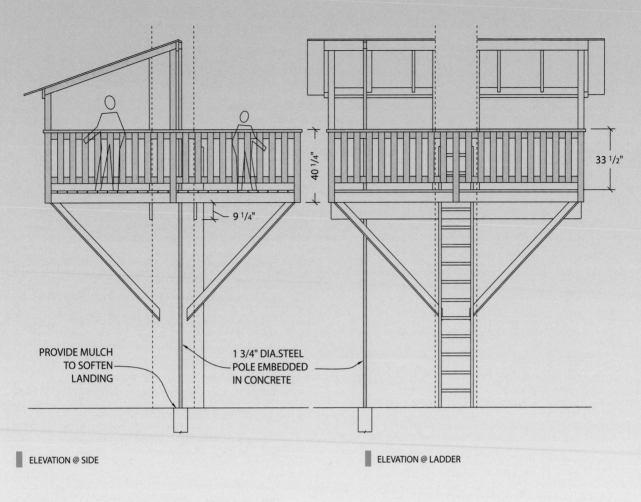

40 1/4"

9 1/4"

33 1/2"

PROVIDE MULCH
TO SOFTEN
LANDING

1 3/4" DIA. STEEL
POLE EMBEDDED
IN CONCRETE

■ ELEVATION @ SIDE

■ ELEVATION @ LADDER

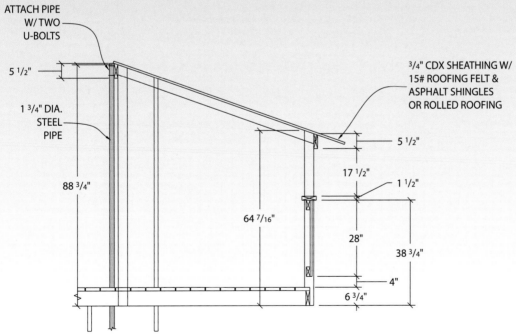

ATTACH PIPE
W/ TWO
U-BOLTS

5 1/2"

1 3/4" DIA.
STEEL
PIPE

88 3/4"

3/4" CDX SHEATHING W/
15# ROOFING FELT &
ASPHALT SHINGLES
OR ROLLED ROOFING

5 1/2"

17 1/2"

1 1/2"

64 7/16"

28"

38 3/4"

4"

6 3/4"

■ SIDE SECTION @ ROOF/RAILING

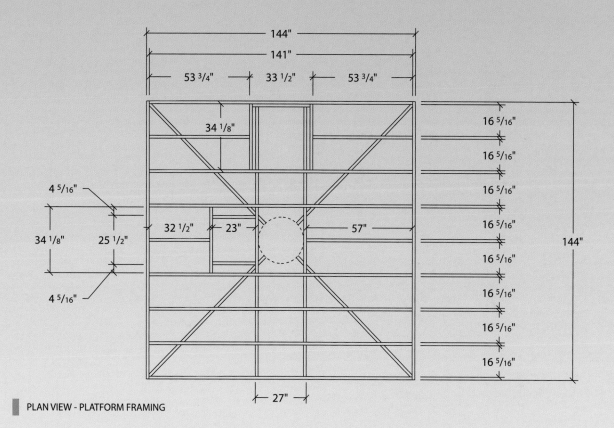

PLAN VIEW - PLATFORM FRAMING

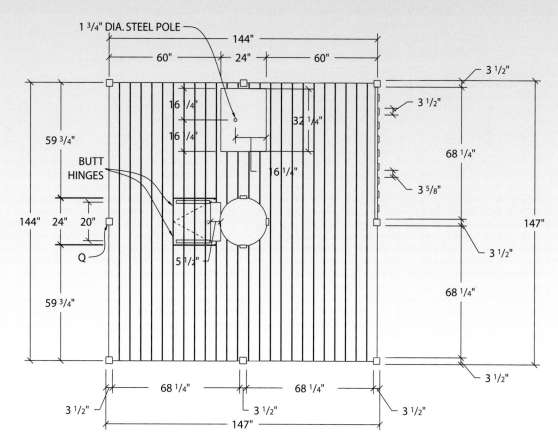

PLAN VIEW - DECKING/RAILING

Plan 4: Wraparound Shed on Stilts

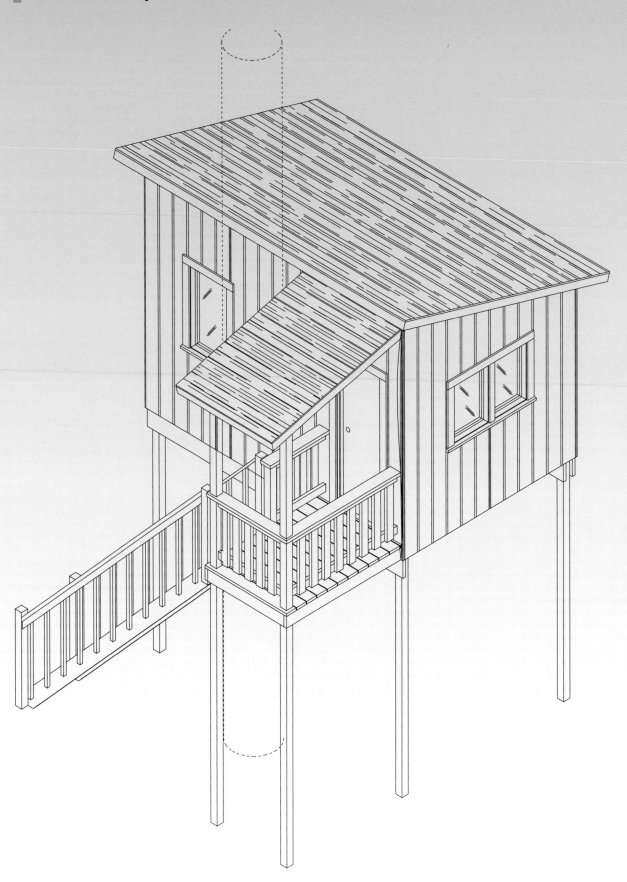

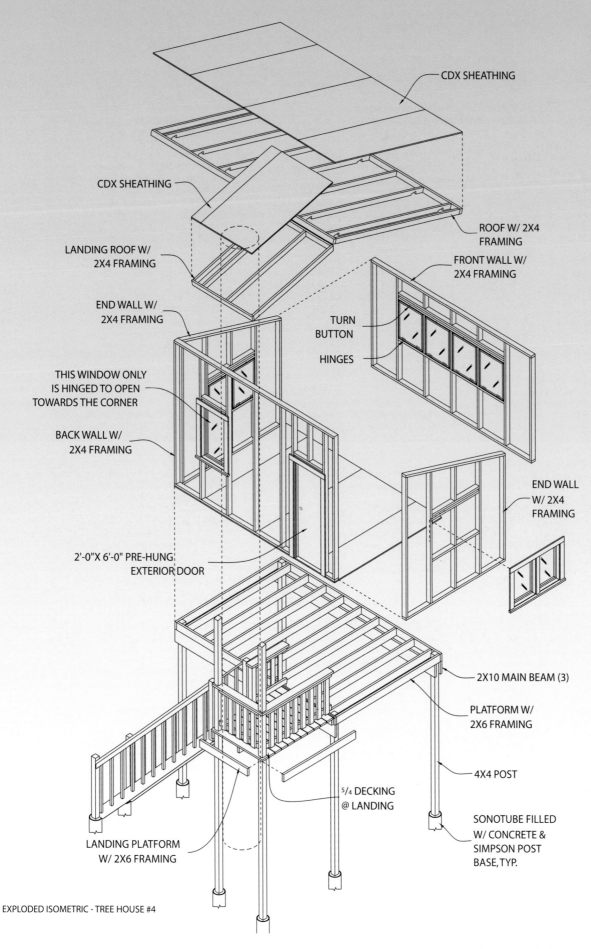

CDX SHEATHING

CDX SHEATHING

LANDING ROOF W/ 2X4 FRAMING

END WALL W/ 2X4 FRAMING

THIS WINDOW ONLY IS HINGED TO OPEN TOWARDS THE CORNER

BACK WALL W/ 2X4 FRAMING

2'-0"X 6'-0" PRE-HUNG EXTERIOR DOOR

ROOF W/ 2X4 FRAMING

FRONT WALL W/ 2X4 FRAMING

TURN BUTTON

HINGES

END WALL W/ 2X4 FRAMING

2X10 MAIN BEAM (3)

PLATFORM W/ 2X6 FRAMING

4X4 POST

⁵/₄ DECKING @ LANDING

SONOTUBE FILLED W/ CONCRETE & SIMPSON POST BASE, TYP.

LANDING PLATFORM W/ 2X6 FRAMING

EXPLODED ISOMETRIC - TREE HOUSE #4

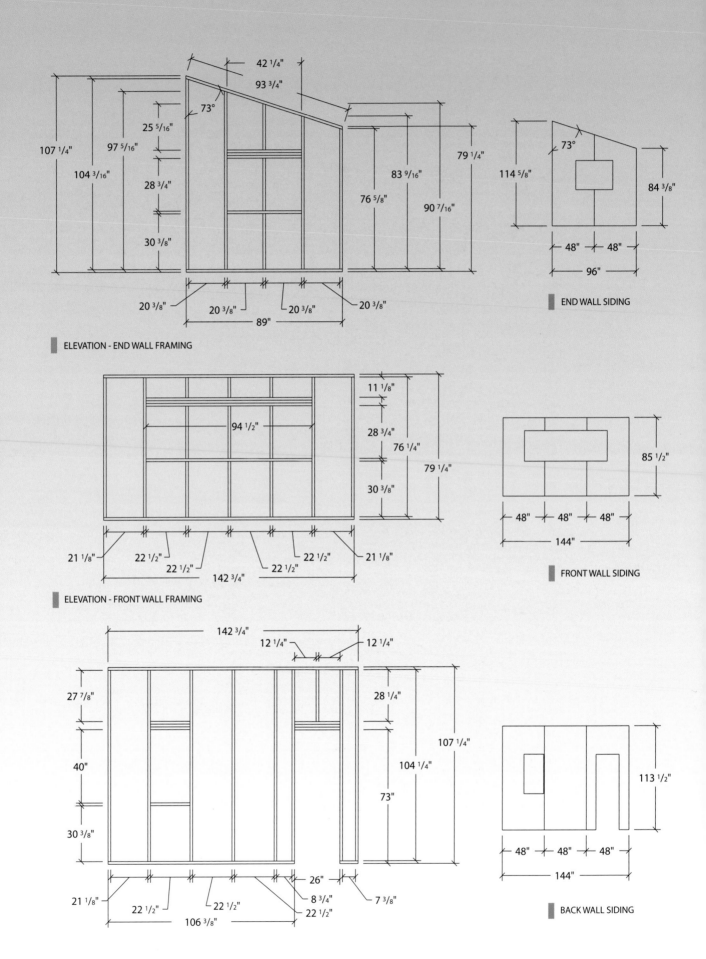

42 1/4"

93 3/4"

73°

107 1/4"

104 3/16"

97 5/16"

25 5/16"

28 3/4"

30 3/8"

83 9/16"

79 1/4"

76 5/8"

90 7/16"

20 3/8"   20 3/8"   20 3/8"   20 3/8"

89"

ELEVATION - END WALL FRAMING

73°

114 5/8"

84 3/8"

48"   48"

96"

END WALL SIDING

94 1/2"

11 1/8"

28 3/4"

76 1/4"

30 3/8"

79 1/4"

21 1/8"   22 1/2"   22 1/2"   22 1/2"   22 1/2"   21 1/8"

142 3/4"

ELEVATION - FRONT WALL FRAMING

85 1/2"

48"   48"   48"

144"

FRONT WALL SIDING

142 3/4"

12 1/4"   12 1/4"

27 7/8"

40"

30 3/8"

28 1/4"

107 1/4"

104 1/4"

73"

21 1/8"   22 1/2"   22 1/2"   26"   8 3/4"   7 3/8"

22 1/2"

106 3/8"

113 1/2"

48"   48"   48"

144"

BACK WALL SIDING

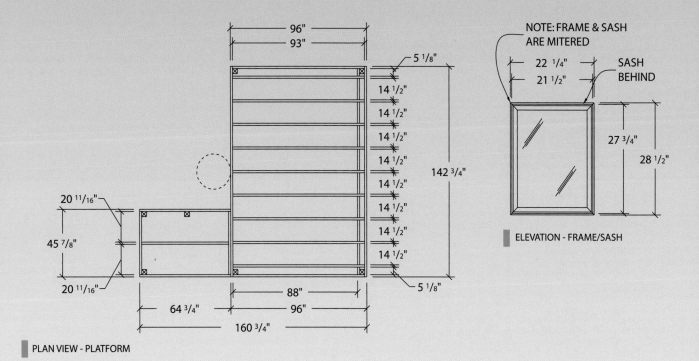

PLAN VIEW - PLATFORM

ELEVATION - FRAME/SASH

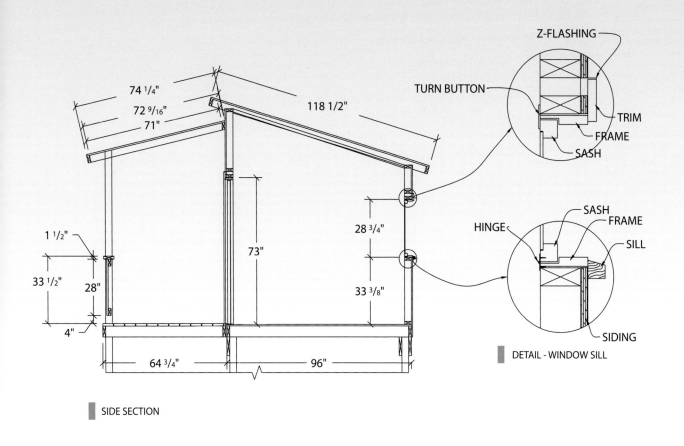

SIDE SECTION

DETAIL - WINDOW SILL

Plan 5: Triangular Tree Hut

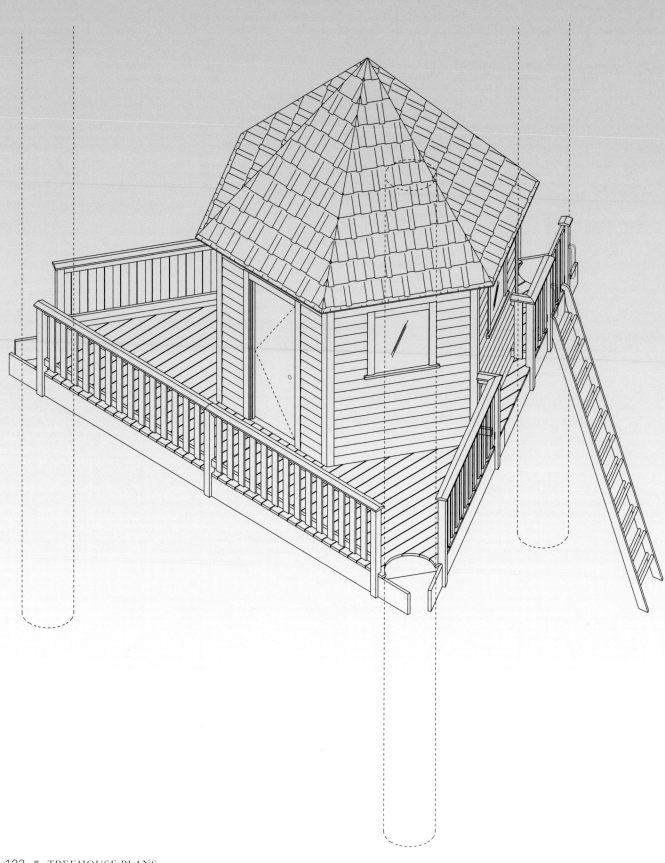

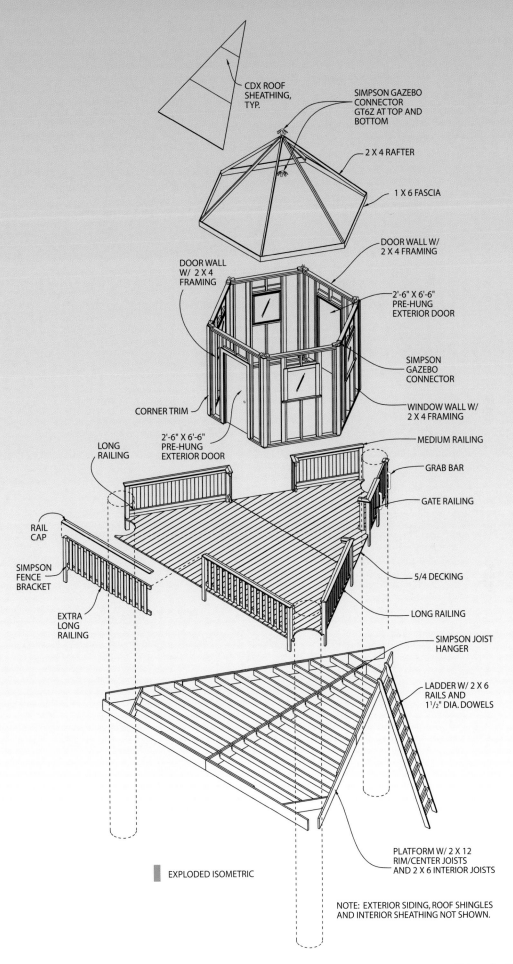

CDX ROOF SHEATHING, TYP.

SIMPSON GAZEBO CONNECTOR GT6Z AT TOP AND BOTTOM

2 X 4 RAFTER

1 X 6 FASCIA

DOOR WALL W/ 2 X 4 FRAMING

DOOR WALL W/ 2 X 4 FRAMING

2'-6" X 6'-6" PRE-HUNG EXTERIOR DOOR

SIMPSON GAZEBO CONNECTOR

CORNER TRIM

WINDOW WALL W/ 2 X 4 FRAMING

2'-6" X 6'-6" PRE-HUNG EXTERIOR DOOR

LONG RAILING

MEDIUM RAILING

GRAB BAR

GATE RAILING

RAIL CAP

SIMPSON FENCE BRACKET

EXTRA LONG RAILING

5/4 DECKING

LONG RAILING

SIMPSON JOIST HANGER

LADDER W/ 2 X 6 RAILS AND 1 1/2" DIA. DOWELS

PLATFORM W/ 2 X 12 RIM/CENTER JOISTS AND 2 X 6 INTERIOR JOISTS

EXPLODED ISOMETRIC

NOTE: EXTERIOR SIDING, ROOF SHINGLES AND INTERIOR SHEATHING NOT SHOWN.

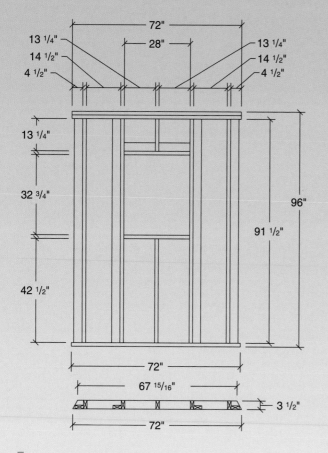

WINDOW WALL FRAMING

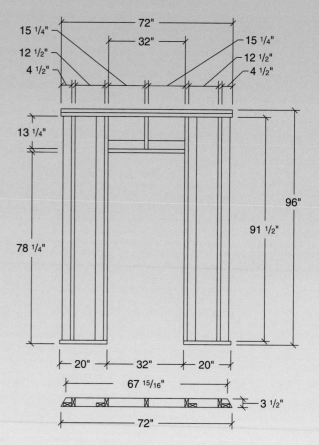

DOOR WALL FRAMING

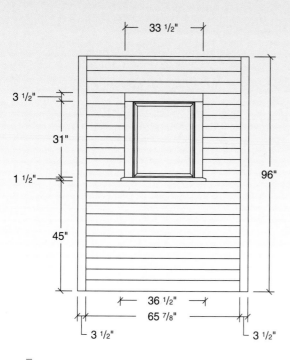

WINDOW WALL TRIM & SIDING

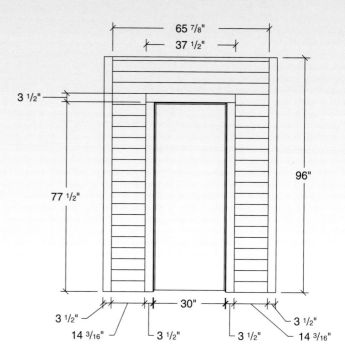

DOOR WALL TRIM & SIDING

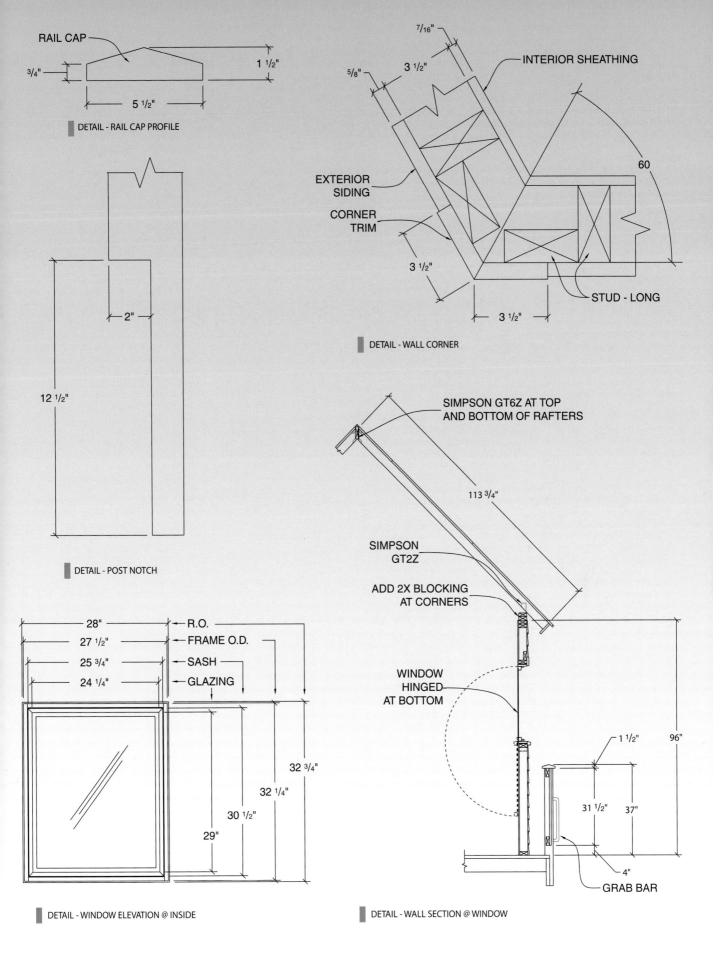

RAIL CAP

3/4"

1 1/2"

5 1/2"

DETAIL - RAIL CAP PROFILE

2"

12 1/2"

DETAIL - POST NOTCH

7/16"

3 1/2"

5/8"

INTERIOR SHEATHING

60

EXTERIOR
SIDING

CORNER
TRIM

3 1/2"

STUD - LONG

3 1/2"

DETAIL - WALL CORNER

SIMPSON GT6Z AT TOP
AND BOTTOM OF RAFTERS

113 3/4"

SIMPSON
GT2Z

ADD 2X BLOCKING
AT CORNERS

WINDOW
HINGED
AT BOTTOM

1 1/2"

96"

31 1/2"

37"

4"

GRAB BAR

28" — R.O.

27 1/2" — FRAME O.D.

25 3/4" — SASH

24 1/4" — GLAZING

32 3/4"

32 1/4"

30 1/2"

29"

DETAIL - WINDOW ELEVATION @ INSIDE

DETAIL - WALL SECTION @ WINDOW

Triangular Tree Hut ■ 135

Plan 6: Four-tree Shanty

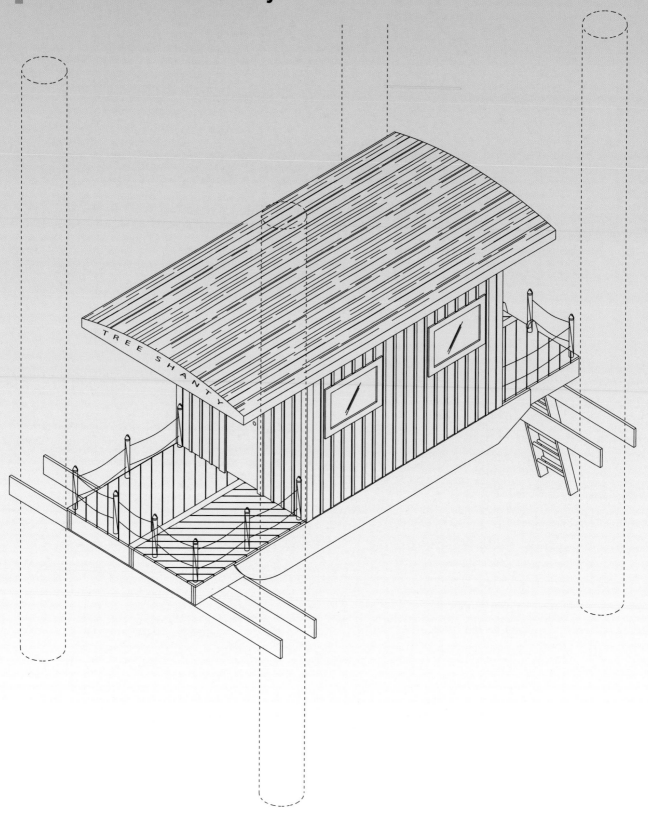

TREE SHANTY

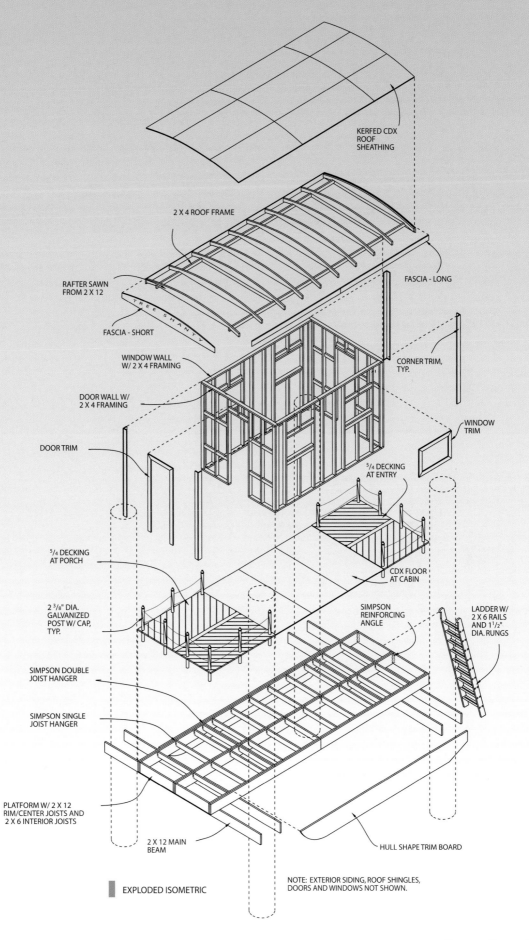

KERFED CDX ROOF SHEATHING

2 X 4 ROOF FRAME

RAFTER SAWN FROM 2 X 12

FASCIA - LONG

FASCIA - SHORT

WINDOW WALL W/ 2 X 4 FRAMING

CORNER TRIM, TYP.

DOOR WALL W/ 2 X 4 FRAMING

DOOR TRIM

WINDOW TRIM

⁵⁄₄ DECKING AT ENTRY

⁵⁄₄ DECKING AT PORCH

CDX FLOOR AT CABIN

2 ³⁄₈" DIA. GALVANIZED POST W/ CAP, TYP.

SIMPSON REINFORCING ANGLE

LADDER W/ 2 X 6 RAILS AND 1¹⁄₂" DIA. RUNGS

SIMPSON DOUBLE JOIST HANGER

SIMPSON SINGLE JOIST HANGER

PLATFORM W/ 2 X 12 RIM/CENTER JOISTS AND 2 X 6 INTERIOR JOISTS

2 X 12 MAIN BEAM

HULL SHAPE TRIM BOARD

NOTE: EXTERIOR SIDING, ROOF SHINGLES, DOORS AND WINDOWS NOT SHOWN.

EXPLODED ISOMETRIC

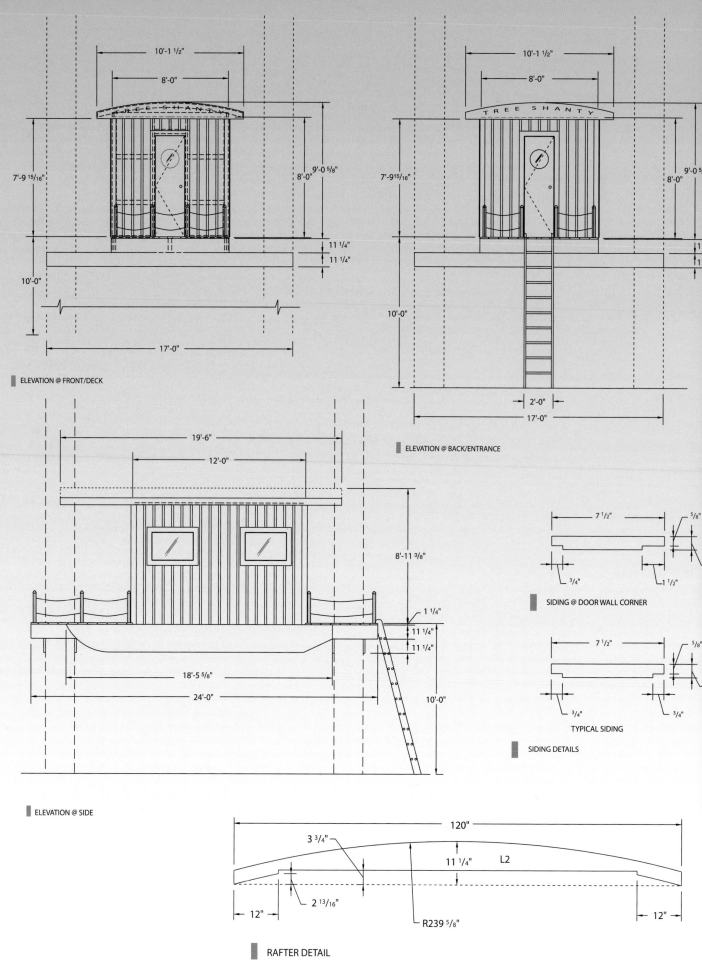

ELEVATION @ FRONT/DECK

ELEVATION @ BACK/ENTRANCE

ELEVATION @ SIDE

SIDING @ DOOR WALL CORNER

TYPICAL SIDING

SIDING DETAILS

RAFTER DETAIL

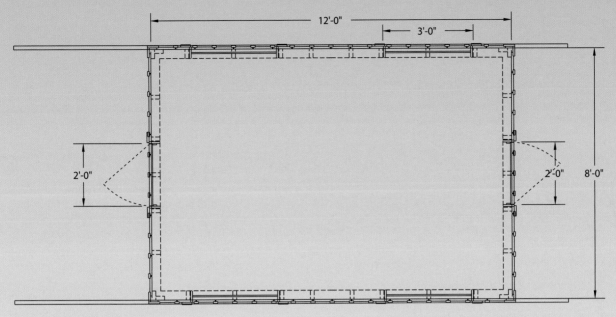

■ PLAN VIEW - WALL FRAMING ONLY

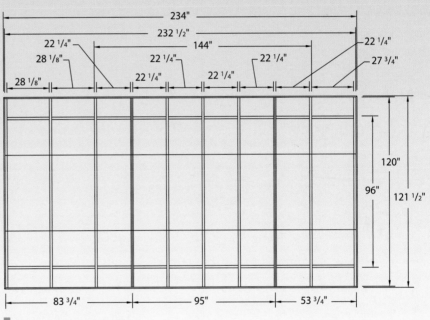

■ PLAN VIEW - ROOF FRAMING

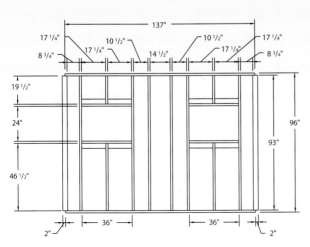

■ WINDOW WALL FRAMING

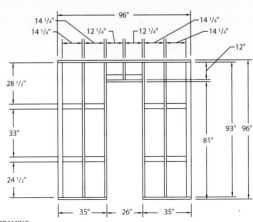

■ DOOR WALL FRAMING

Resources

Black & Decker
Portable power tools
www.blackanddecker.com
800-544-6986

Bracketree©
Garnier Limb© tree brackets
www.treehouses.com/treehouse/
construction/bracketree.html
541-592-2208

Fehr Bros. Industries
Hardware (cables, ties, etc.) for trees:
http://store.treecarehardware.com/
index.html
800-598-5437
e-mail: treecare@fehr.com

**National Resource Center for
Health and Safety in Child Care**
Recommendations for ground covers
under play equipment
http://nrc.uchsc.edu/CFOC/HTMLVer-
sion/Appendix_V.html
800-598-5437

Simpson Strong-Tie
Lumber connector hardware
www.strongtie.com
800-999-5099

The Treehouse Guide
On-line treehouse information and links
www.thetreehouseguide.com

Through the Roof
Clear roof sealant (p. 103)
Sashco, Inc.
www.sashcosealants.com
800-289-7290

Photo Credits

PHOTOGRAPHERS

Alamy
www.alamy.com
page 10 (bottom) ©Nina Buesing/Alamy;
page13 (top right) ©Paul Bradforth/Alamy.

Barbara Butler Artist-Builder, Inc.
www.barbarabutler.com
San Francisca, CA
The following photos and tree house designs are
©Barbara Butler Artist-Builder: pages 6, 7 (top),
16 (bottom), 112, 113 (left), 114-115 (all).

Photolibrary Group Ltd.
pages 8, 9 (top left and top right), 11 (bottom left and
top): © Juliette Wade/ Garden Picture Library/ Photo-
library.com.

page 11 (bottom right): © Mark Bolton/ Garden Picture
Library/ Photolibrary.com.

page 17 (bottom): © Ann Cutting/ Botanica/ Photo-
library.com.

Mary Martin
© Mary Martin. Istockphoto.com: page 7 (bottom)

Sergio Piumatti
Richardson, TX
©Sergio Piumatti: pages 12 (both), 13 (top left, bottom).

Andrea Rugg
Minneapolis, MN
©Andrea Rugg: pages 9 (bottom), 10 (top), 16 (top),
17 (top)

Jessie Walker
www.jessiewalker.com
©Jessie Walker: pages 14 (bottom), 15 (both).

Index

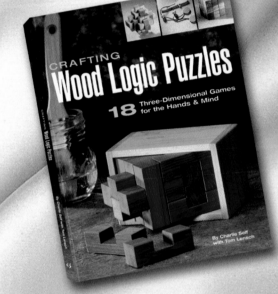
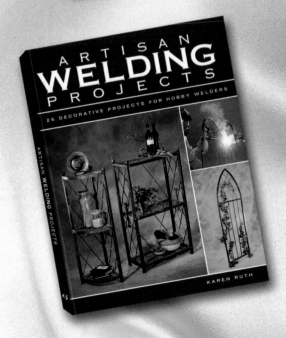

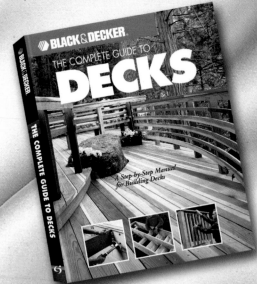
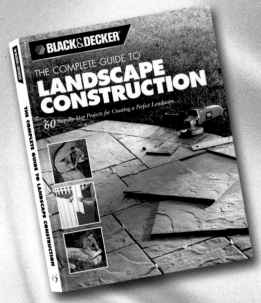